THE SHIRLEY TEMPLE STORY

Other Books by Lester David

THE LONELY LADY OF SAN CLEMENTE:
THE STORY OF PAT NIXON

SECOND SIGHT

TED KENNEDY: TRIUMPHS AND TRAGEDIES

JOAN, THE RELUCTANT KENNEDY

ETHEL: THE STORY OF MRS. ROBERT F. KENNEDY

JACKIE AND ARI (WITH JHAN ROBBINS)

RICHARD AND ELIZABETH (WITH JHAN ROBBINS)

IKE AND MAMIE:
THE STORY OF THE GENERAL AND HIS LADY
(WITH IRENE DAVID)

The Shirley Temple Story

Lester David
and Irene David

G. P. Putnam's Sons   New York

Library of Congress Cataloging in Publication Data

David, Lester.
  The Shirley Temple story.

  Filmography: p.
  Bibliography: p.
  Includes index.
  1. Temple, Shirley, 1928–   . 2. Moving-
picture actors and actresses—United States—
Biography.   I. David, Irene.   II. Title.
PN2287.T33D3   1982   791.43'028'0924   [B]   82-15027
ISBN 0-399-12798-4

Acknowledgments

We wish to express special thanks to many persons who shared their thoughts and recollections with us and answered our endless questions. We are indebted more than we can say to President Ronald Reagan, who took time from an extraordinarily busy day to talk about his former co-star. We extend gratitude beyond measure to those grand veterans of the early years whose memories of Shirley Temple are still fresh and green—particularly Jay Gorney, who discovered her, and Abe Katz, who made the first doll. Patriarchs of the I-worked-with-Shirley group include directors Henry Hathaway and Allan Dwan; their gracious cooperation is deeply appreciated. (Sadly, Allan Dwan, who was ninety-six when he talked to us, passed away before this book could be published.)

Thanks, too, to the many stars, child actors, chroniclers of Hollywood and others who worked with her, including Rudy Vallee, Jackie Cooper, Jane Withers, Senator George Murphy, Louis Sobol, Sidney Skolsky, Harriet Parsons, Dorothy Manners, Gene Reynolds, Paul MacNamara, Delmar Watson and so many others. For his gracious cooperation, we extend special appreciation to John Agar.

Immeasurably helpful were the librarians at the Academy of Motion Picture Arts and Science in Los Angeles, the Lincoln Center Library for the Performing Arts in New York City, the American Film Institute in Washington, the Film Study Center of the Museum of Modern Art in New York, the Oral History Research Office at Columbia University, and the Franklin D. Roosevelt Library at Hyde Park. *Movie Star News* was most helpful in locating early Temple photos.

In Washington, we obtained much valuable help from the Foreign Service Institute of the U.S. State Department and from Victor

Gold. In the San Francisco area, our thanks go to Dave Schutz, the retired managing editor of the *Redwood City Tribune*, now the *Peninsula Times-Tribune*, the staff of the Stanford University Medical Center in Palo Alto and all the librarians of all the newspapers and communities who gave unstintingly of their time to help us find material. Our appreciation goes to all the journalists there who helped, too numerous to name all, though we must mention Harry Farrell of the *San Jose Mercury*. In Los Angeles, we are grateful to the kind people at the Screen Actors Guild, the Directors Guild of America, the staff of the Westlake School for Girls, and all the grips, electricians and other technicians who worked on Temple movies and remembered.

The Ideal Toy Corporation and the members of the still-active, still-enthusiastic Shirley Temple fan clubs deserve a deep bow for their assistance. Surely not the least, we thank Professor William Everson and film expert Meade Roberts. Thanks to Professor Everson, we were able to view those Temple movies we were unable to catch on television.

Woodmere, New York LESTER DAVID and IRENE DAVID

To the "old" movies,
which, imperfect though they were, helped lift
the spirits of a more imperfect world

Contents

The Shirley Temple phenomenon began a half century ago, in 1933, in the midst of the Great Depression. It remains unequaled in the history of entertainment. Looking back on this golden anniversary, it seems startling that the country, indeed the world, would be bowled over by a little girl, yet it happened and this is the story.

Part One
THE ENCHANTED YEARS

1

The Importance of Being Shirley

A statuette of Shirley Temple stood for years on a pedestal just inside the entrance of the small, austere lobby of the 20th Century–Fox, Inc., administration building off West Pico Boulevard in Los Angeles.

Each morning, when the staff people reported for work, it was the custom for everyone, from file clerks to major executives, to pause and bow reverently before the little idol.

With appropriate symbolism, the figure was painted gold: before Shirley came on the scene, the studio was edging close to bankruptcy; she pulled it out of danger. "If there had not been a Shirley Temple," said a company executive years later, "there would not be a 20th Century–Fox today."

The statuette disappeared during a recent refurbishing, but the impact she had endured after fifty years.

She was five when the fairy-tale life began, and before she was ten she had captivated hundreds of millions around the world, including at least ten heads of state and a number of others who would one day rule their nations.

She corresponded with President Franklin D. Roosevelt, who answered her letters promptly. Soon after he took office for his first term in the gloomy 1930s, Roosevelt declared: "When the spirit of the people is lower than at any other time during this Depression, it is a splendid thing that for just fifteen cents an American can go to a movie and look at the smiling face of a baby and forget his troubles."

Arturo Alessandri, the President of Chile, ordered every one of her movies shown at his official residence in Santiago as soon as each was released. In his enchantment, he suggested that the Chilean Navy name her its official mascot, which it did. Next, Alessandri decided she needed a uniform for the post. Secretly, he sent to Hollywood for her measurements and had his official tailors sew for Shirley a special uniform as admiral of the fleet. When it was finished, he dispatched a courier to Los Angeles to deliver the uniform personally.

In the Ukraine, a stocky, roundheaded little man, rising to prominence in the region's Communist Party, had little interest in movies except when Shirley Temple pictures were shown. Then he went to see every one. Many years later, Nikita S. Khrushchev, by now the Premier of the Soviet Union, made his unprecedented thirteen-day tour of the United States, arriving in San Francisco on September 20, 1960. Shirley Temple, a grown woman of thirty-two, stood in the receiving line at a reception in his honor. Not recognizing her, he shook hands, mumbled a greeting, and turned to the next distinguished guest. An aide whispered something quickly in Khrushchev's ear, and his face lit up. Turning, he spun Shirley around and smiled at her. "His eyes got teary," Shirley said. "He grabbed my two hands and pumped them against his stomach." He was overjoyed at meeting her.

When England's Queen Elizabeth was ten years old and her sister Margaret Rose seven, they insisted on showing Shirley's movies at their birthday parties.

Add President Ronald Reagan to the list of heads of state who are numbered among her fans. He remembers her well, and with deep affection.

On April 11, 1981, the telephone rang in our home shortly after three in the afternoon. The White House was calling. President Reagan, the operator said, would be on the line in a moment.

We had earlier requested an interview with the President, who had been one of Shirley Temple's co-stars during his acting years, but we were mindful of all the problems that month. Argentina had invaded the Falkland Islands, the Middle East was boiling again, the Administration and Congressional leaders were locked in battle over the budget.

However, within a few minutes, we were speaking to the President.

"I would love to see you and talk about Shirley," he said, "but I guess you know my schedule. Can I write you something about her?"

"Certainly, Mr. President. Would you have just a moment now to share some of your memories of Shirley with us?"

He agreed, and the "moment" stretched into almost fifteen minutes. Ronald Reagan said he had not wanted to see Shirley grow up. Along with millions of Americans, he cherished his recollections of her moppet years and wanted to halt time in its flight. Yet he was the one who had had to present her to America and the world for the first time as a young lady.

"We became acquainted," he said, "when she was borrowed by Warner Brothers and we co-starred in a picture called *That Hagen Girl*, somewhere around 1947. It was the story of an older man and a young girl. "I was the first person to say, 'I love you, will you marry me?' to Shirley Temple in the movies, but it was a most embarrassing experience."

In the movie Shirley, who was then nineteen years old, played the role of Mary Hagen, an illegitimate child who has been adopted by a small-town Ohio family and has grown up suffering snubs and gossip from malicious neighbors. Reagan, in the part of Tom Bates, a returning war hero, is suspected of being Shirley's father, and throughout most of the picture she believes he is, though she never lets on. At length, after many complications, Mary confronts Tom for the truth of his relationship to her and Tom denies the story. No, he is not her father. Predictably, the two fall in love.

Now the President continues the story. "At the sneak preview when the picture was finished, I was in the theater. When that moment came on the screen and I spoke that 'I love you' line, there was a loud chorus from the audience of '*Oh, No!*' The scene was later taken out of the film."

Reagan said he shrank down in his seat and would not leave the theater until the audience had filed out. To him the incident revealed that moviegoers cherished their recollections of the moppet years deeply.

"She was conscious of the fact that audiences were unwilling to let her grow up," he said. "She wanted very much to be accepted as an adult actress carrying on in the profession which had been hers for so long. I never let her know that, having been a part of that audience, I wasn't quite ready, either, and not so sure that I wanted to be a party to presenting her to America for the first time as a young lady."

But, the President said, she was indeed that—"a lady in every sense of the word."

He admired her, too, for her exceptional talent. "Shirley was a trouper, a real professional," Mr. Reagan said. "One of her movies, I can't recall which it was, called for a sad scene in which she had to sob as though her heart was breaking. She did it so well, so convincingly, that by the time she was finished almost everyone on the set was weeping, too.

"When the director said, 'Cut,' ending the scene, Shirley walked to the center of the set, bowed to the cast and crew and said, 'Next week, *East Lynne.*'" (Shirley was using a show-business catch phrase which referred to an old-time tear-jerking melodrama, a favorite of traveling stock companies, whose managers would appear before the curtain to announce what was coming: "Next week, *East Lynne.*")

"Shirley Temple gave us a great deal of joy in our time," the President concluded. "No one has equaled her."

Will there ever be another Shirley Temple?

Ronald Reagan doesn't think so. "I see some very talented youngsters now," the President said, "but there is nothing to develop them. In those days, we were a family. The studios trained actors and actresses, brought them along and helped them grow. That's gone now."

In today's Hollywood, the President said, an actor or actress is engaged for a role, performs it, then leaves to find something else at another studio. With the abandonment of the studio system, with its coaches and contract-player arrangements, the performer has far less opportunity to learn his or her craft.

A few days later, as he had promised, President Reagan amplified his comments in a special statement to us.

"Like everyone else in America," he said, "I loved Shirley Temple in those days when a depression-haunted world forgot the drab dreariness for a few hours in a neighborhood movie house, especially when a tiny golden-haired girl named Shirley Temple was on the screen. Her talent and ability were such that at one time rumors went around that she was much older than she was said to be, and was somehow stunted in her growth. This was so patently ridiculous that little credence was given to it. But affection for her probably helped, too. She was a beloved American institution, and people wouldn't hold still for any attempt to deprecate her. . . . Let me just say that she was totally unspoiled, with a delightful sense of humor. She was most likable and in theater language a real pro. She was also intelligent, well informed, and with an interest in a wide range of subjects."

Shirley Temple outdrew such towering film favorites as Clark Gable, Greta Garbo, James Cagney, Humphrey Bogart, Spencer Tracy, Joan Crawford and Marlene Dietrich. For four successive years, from 1935 to 1938, she was the number-one box-office attraction in the U.S.. Only Bing Crosby, who was top earner five years in a row in the following decade, has ever beaten that record. "All the Garbos and the Gables, the Colberts and the Lombards together," marveled the writer J. P. McAvoy, "can't pull them into the theaters the way Shirley does. And that goes for not only this country but for every country in the world. Whatever she's got, it sells better than glamour, romance, adventure, comedy, tragedy or sex."

The importance of the forty-two pound, forty-five-inch-tall little girl to the world of high finance was brought home to a leading screenwriter of the times in 1935 when the Fox Film Corporation merged with 20th Century. Shirley, who had started her career at

Fox, came with the deal. To celebrate the union of the two studios, a formal dinner was held in the grand ballroom of a Beverly Hills hotel. Wall Street tycoons and bankers came from the East Coast, a three-day train journey, to join studio executives and stars at the head table. Among the guests were Will Rogers, Janet Gaynor, Warner Baxter and Warner Oland, the original portrayer of Charlie Chan, along with lesser luminaries, directors and writers.

Just before the speeches began, Shirley skipped in. As she passed the table of screenwriter Sam Hellman, he reached out, took her hand and spun her around. Hellman, who worked for Fox, had feared with some justification that his job was in peril. A bit giddy with delight that the merger spared him from the ax, at least for a while, and perhaps having had a few heady drafts of champagne as well, he stood and lifted her high over his head. Holding her at arm's length, he told her how happy he was, how well she acted and how successful they all would be.

Relating the story, Hellman said, "Suddenly a horrible silence fell on the room, and I looked toward the head table. There all the bankers from New York had turned white and were mopping big drops of sweat from their brows. I realized then what I was doing. Here I was holding practically all the assets of 20th Century–Fox in my hands. It scared me so I nearly dropped her. But I managed to set her on the floor, and when I looked at the head table again the bankers were sighing big sighs of relief and the color was creeping back into their faces."

One morning Darryl F. Zanuck, the head of production at 20th Century, was conferring with John Steinbeck on the screenplay of *The Grapes of Wrath,* which was to become one of the all-time great films and would vault Henry Fonda to stardom. A secretary buzzed from the outer office. The imperious Zanuck never allowed interruptions, except for crisis. This was a crisis.

"Mr. Zanuck, Mr. Zanuck!" the secretary sputtered. "There's been an accident on one of our sets."

"What happened?" Zanuck bellowed.

"Shirley Temple has lost her tooth, and—"

Zanuck, Steinbeck noted, paled. "Her *front* tooth?" he wanted to know.

"It was," the secretary replied.

Zanuck made a quick executive decision. "Tell them to get the best dentist," he barked, adding, "and close down the company."

So, on the set of *The Little Princess,* director Walter Lang ordered the lights turned off and the cameras to stop grinding on the $1.5-million movie, a huge budget for the times. Cesar Romero, Arthur Treacher, Richard Greene, Anita Louise and the rest of the cast and crew sat around idly while Shirley was rushed to a dentist to have a replacement made.

During the excitement Steinbeck told Zanuck, with heavy sarcasm, "Don't bother about me, *The Grapes of Wrath* is unimportant compared to Shirley Temple's tooth."

Considering the potential financial returns of the two properties at the time, he was probably right.

Women around the country not only flocked to see Shirley in the movies but were eager to have a child like her. Along with the hundreds of thousands of fan letters which came to the studio's mail room each year were thousands of others addressed to her father, George. Shirley's mother, Gertrude, was tall and slender and quite unlike her daughter, but George was short, plump, cherubic, usually smiling and similarly dimpled. The resemblance was strong and did not go unnoticed, and George received countless offers from women who wanted, with his help, a Shirley of their own.

"Naturally enough," said a former publicist, "George Temple was proud as a bantam rooster when he read all those invitations, but Gertrude was furious. She gave orders to the mail room to have all such letters sent directly to the fan mail department, where they would be routinely answered with noncommittal notes. George was sorry about that. They had spiced up his life a little."

Most little girls of her generation wanted to look and behave like Shirley, even the youthful Jayne Mansfield. In Bryn Mawr, Pennsylvania, Jayne (born Vera Jayne Palmer) went to all her movies, learned all her songs and considered Shirley her "ideal." When she entered her teens, Jayne was still dressing like Shirley and imitating her, though by that time she had a bust no brassiere could adequately ensnare. Wrote Martha Sexton, Mansfield's biographer: "Jayne aped Shirley Temple's innocence and wound up acting like jailbait."

Honors were heaped upon Shirley from practically everywhere. The state of Kentucky breveted her a colonel, the then territory of Hawaii conferred the same rank upon her in its National Guard, and the Texas Rangers made her a captain. As the Temple craze careened along, the Boy Scouts of America were so carried away that, overlooking gender, they sent her a badge and a kerchief and told her she was one of them. In Scotland, the 400,000-member Chums' Club, a children's organization, elected her its president, while in England the 165,000 youngsters of the Kiddies Club did the same. The entire Kiddies membership took an oath to follow faithfully the example she set in character, behavior and personal manners.

She was named honorary chairman of practically everything from Be Kind to Animals Week to National Air Mail Week. She took the latter post, bestowed by Postmaster General James A. Farley, seriously. Between scenes, she painted a poster of an airplane which resembled a large fish more than it did a flying machine, drew herself standing in the foreground and sent it off to Washington. Canny Jim Farley, who could spot a good publicity gimmick when he saw one, had the Temple art reproduced and circulated all across the country.

The phenomenon grew as she went from film to film. When she fell ill one year, twenty thousand people on the island of Bali in Indonesia gathered on a vast field and fell to their knees in prayer for her recovery. A Japanese movie magazine published two successive issues filled only with her photographs and sold a million copies of each one even though there was not one word of description or explanation; none was needed. Her fan clubs proliferated around the world, so fast nobody ever kept count of their numbers. According to one estimate, their total membership was four million, far more than any other star of the times. More than twelve thousand requests for her autographed picture came to the studio every month. She was one of the first of the poster girls; a three-foot likeness of her as she appeared in *Little Miss Marker* was bought by the tens of thousands. When she wore a special kind of bow in her hair in a film, the ribbon industry couldn't keep up with the demand from parents and little girls.

The appeal has been universal and it has lasted. To this day, a drink named after her is served to children while their parents drink harder stuff. The original Shirley Temple drink: pour a half ounce of grenadine over ice in a highball glass, fill with ginger ale and top with a cherry. Over the years, bars and restaurants have fancied up the recipe. One calls for grenadine, three ounces of ginger ale, a similar amount of orange juice, a cherry, a wedge of lime and an orange slice, all over crushed ice. Another version is served in a champagne glass. In San Francisco, the drink is called a Mrs. Charles Black. Another variation is a Shirley Temple Black, made with a cola drink. The concoction has followed Shirley through life. In restaurants, strangers often ask waiters to bring her one as a joke. "I can't stand the thing," she says. "It's too sweet and icky." She prefers tomato juice.

A "Shirley Temple amendment" to the Wages and Hours Law, barring the sale of any products that are manufactured by children under sixteen, is on the statute books. In 1975, the Food and Agricultural Organization of the United Nations put her name and likeness on its Ceres Medals, and in the following year telephone directories in a number of states bore a drawing of her.

And just before Thanksgiving of 1981, Secretary of State Alexander M. Haig, Jr., disclosed that his personal heroes were Winston Churchill, Douglas MacArthur and Dwight D. Eisenhower, the movie he liked best was *Gone With the Wind*—and his favorite actress of all time was Shirley Temple.

2

"How do you make a Shirley Temple?"

In 1962, Abe Katz, who was in charge of fashioning and manufacturing the first Shirley Temple doll, was given a testimonial dinner at the Plaza Hotel in New York. Abe, short, slender and natty in a new tuxedo, was celebrating his fiftieth anniversary with the Ideal Toy Corporation, which made the doll and still reissues it periodically. Recalling the problems he faced, he told the audience, "Believe me, I had many sleepless nights in those days trying to figure out how to make a Shirley Temple."

Seated nearby at the head table was Shirley herself, then in her middle thirties. When she heard Abe's confession she called out, "So did my mother!"

The quip brought down the house, but it was more than an off-the-cuff line. Shirley's mother, Gertrude, was a key factor in shaping the life and career of her daughter. She was mainly responsible for training her, bringing her to the attention of people who counted, and guiding her along the perilous path of child stardom. She did it shrewdly, never once admitting it was her intention; yet it is clear that she wanted the best and biggest for her daughter and, in her quiet yet forceful way, managed to get it.

Allan Dwan, who directed three Temple films, says, "Without

Gertrude, who knew what to do and when to do it, there would have been no Temple phenomenon." Paul MacNamara, public-relations director of Richard Selznick Studios, who, as a young publicist, worked closely with mother and daughter, declares, "Gertrude was the works. She was smart enough to realize from the very first that her daughter had enormous potential. She got Shirley into films and made sure her career progressed at exactly the right pace, slowly and naturally, growing and strengthening year by year. She knew that if she rushed her too fast, the little girl would have peaked into a too-early stardom she could not handle and would have disappeared into oblivion."

Shirley's mother, Gertrude Amelia Krieger, was born in Elgin, Illinois, in 1894, the eldest child of a jeweler who had learned his trade in Germany and immigrated to America as a young man. Soon after she was born, her father moved his family, two sons and a daughter, to Chicago, where before long his business faltered and came to a dead stop. Krieger, seeking to make a new start elsewhere, became fascinated with the young state of California, where new industries were springing up and population was rapidly rising.

A tidal wave of settlers had flooded the area in the mid-1880s when a land boom began, swelling the population from twelve thousand to fifty thousand in just two years. The bubble burst but inflated again the following decade and, surprising everyone, kept growing bigger.

Clearly, opportunity called loudly, and Krieger heard. Shortly after the century turned, he closed his business and took his family to Los Angeles. Then as now, it was "nineteen suburbs in search of a city," as the local joke went, a string of communities sprawled over 451 square miles. The boom had lured a crazy quilt of humanity: speculators in search of a quick fortune, the elderly a haven, cultists of every persuasion, readers of palms and tea leaves, and healers who promised everything. A dentist who called himself Painless Parker hired showgirls, attired them in nurses' garb, revealingly tight, and used them to distract patients as he yanked their teeth. The Colony of Unlimited Life posted this schedule for

26

its live-in adherents: rise at 3 A.M., breakfast on a few dried prunes, then head out "to the high places and, for one hour, hold steadfast the thought of Love."

Krieger found a small apartment near downtown Los Angeles and opened a jewelry shop which began to do well almost at once. But only five years after its arrival the family was wrenched by a tragedy. Krieger fell ill, and in 1908 he died.

Gertrude, tall, olive-skinned and exceptionally pretty, was fourteen years old and a student at Polytechnic High School. Suddenly she found herself, with her mother, the main support of the family. She took odd jobs after school and on weekends, and somehow they managed, though not too well. There were bad times, days when food was scarce, but in later years Gertrude never cared to talk about them.

Considering the hardships of her own young girlhood, one need not probe too deeply into her psyche to understand why she determined early on to create a better life for her own daughter. Nor is it any surprise that, at the age of seventeen, Gertrude, seeking the security of a home and family of her own, got married.

In 1911 she became the wife of George Francis Temple, who had arrived in California eight years earlier, also on the tide of new settlers. Born in the small town of Fairview near the shore of Lake Erie, Temple came from a Pennsylvania Dutch family of bankers, doctors and lawyers. Later, when the eighteen-foot-high image of George's little girl began filling the movie screens, amazement swept the community and the family. To the south of Fairview, George's Aunt Sally Mercer, whose ancestors founded the city that bears her name, spoke for them all when she said, "It must be that queer California climate has affected George and Gertrude."

George was then twenty-four years old, a quiet young man with a sunny disposition. Stocky, inches shorter than his wife, he had a respectable job as a teller of the California Bank's branch at Washington Street and Vermont Avenue in Los Angeles.

Five years later they had a son, whom they named John and ever after called Jack. In 1920 George Junior, who went through all of his life as Sonny, was born. By then, George Senior had received several promotions and could afford a small one-story stucco bungalow, painted white with an orange tile roof, at 948 Twenty-fourth Street in Santa Monica, a seaside city built on a high mesa sixteen miles from Los Angeles.

There was an elegant side to Santa Monica. Celebrated film stars such as Charlie Chaplin, Douglas Fairbanks, Mary Pickford and Roscoe "Fatty" Arbuckle came regularly to the attractive bay-front area to dine at the posh café which the comedian Nat C. Goodwin had opened at the end of the Santa Monica pier. But the lives of George and Gertrude never touched those of the moneyed and famous. They were solidly middle-class. Their house had a small back yard, a large mortgage and, on the grassy strip in front, a lone birch tree which had been tilted at a forty-degree angle by the Santa Ana winds and had grown up leaning. In the driveway was George's pride, a large and shiny Graham-Paige sedan. Gertrude planted flowers and vegetables in her yard and tended to them as she watched over her growing boys.

Gertrude wanted a daughter. This time unwilling to leave a thing so important to chance, she sought out ways to influence nature. One doctor she questioned on the subject told her that if her husband had his tonsils removed, she would give birth to a little girl.

She rushed home and told George, who was skeptical, but Gertrude insisted and she prevailed. George went to a hospital and had them taken out. Unfortunately, they grew back. Gertrude told him he must try again. George, this time more reluctantly, agreed to have them excised a second time, and they stayed out.

Gertrude believed that a mother can have a strong effect on her unborn child's nature and abilities, a theory in vogue at the time. She felt that if she would expose herself to all things artistic and aesthetic during her pregnancy, somehow, in some way, the appreciation of these qualities, and of course the talent for them, would be transmitted to the developing infant.

Accordingly, she listened to good music by the hour, studied great paintings and gazed at the beauties of nature. When the little girl became a box-office sensation, Gertrude was pretty much certain her efforts were rewarded. In 1934 she declared, "Perhaps this prenatal preparation helped make Shirley what she is today." Gertrude's conviction could have been reinforced by the fact that when Shirley was only eight months old she would stand in her crib whenever she heard music and wiggle her toes in an effort to dance. "When she was two," said Gertrude, "she began to display a rare sense of rhythm and would keep time with her feet to the music of the radio."

Shirley Jane, six and a half pounds in weight and twenty inches long, with hair that looked blond and eyes that were definitely brown, was delivered by the Temple family physician, Dr. Leo J. Madsen, at exactly 9 P.M. on April 23, 1928. Gertrude was ecstatic, and George, now nearly forty and the manager of the branch bank, reached into the bottom drawer of his desk for the customary box of cigars he had purchased the day before and started handing them out to employees and customers.

Two weeks later, George polished his car, drove to the hospital and brought home his wife and new daughter. Shirley was placed in Sonny's old bassinet which had been stored away and was now brought out into the living room. She slept there, across the room from the five-tube battery-powered radio, with octagonal loud-speaker on top, for which George had paid $175. There was no piano in the room—that would come later—but there was a Victrola with a hinged cover which lifted to expose the turntable, and a handle which had to be cranked to spin it. In a cabinet beneath it were records, carefully slipped into albums, of the classical music Gertrude had played over and over through the winter and early spring, as well as the popular favorites of the day, "Life Is Just a Bowl of Cherries," "Star Dust" and "Night and Day."

Gertrude played the radio and the phonograph even more often now, and she was certain Shirley responded to the music. "She looked like a little dancer," Gertrude recalled, "even as a baby. She was the only infant I ever saw who had pretty legs at birth. Both of my boys had straight-up-and-down legs, but Shirley had dainty calves and delicately turned ankles.

"She began to walk when she was one year old, as most children do. It was then that the most extraordinary thing appeared in her. She walked on her toes. From the time she took her first step, she ran on her toes, as if she were dancing."

*   *   *

Shirley arrived in boom times. Calvin Coolidge was ending what most people felt was a great Presidency, and all signs appeared to prove it. Prosperity had soared to unprecedented levels, the national income was rising steadily, and, although prices were high, wages were keeping pace. Eight months earlier, on August 2, Coolidge had slipped reporters a note containing the single sentence "I do not choose to run," but everyone was convinced the prosperity would surely continue under his successor.

The country was still on an emotional high over the heroic feat of the "Lone Eagle," twenty-five-year-old Captain Charles A. Lindbergh, who had flown solo across the Atlantic eleven months earlier in his single engine *Spirit of St. Louis*. A few months later a young settlement worker named Amelia Earhart became the first woman to fly the Atlantic as a passenger; soon she would fly it alone. In 1928, the eight-hundred-foot *Graf Zeppelin*, carrying fifty passengers, arrived at Lakehurst, New Jersey, from Germany, the first commercial airliner to cross the ocean.

The golden age of sports was at its most gilded stage. Babe Ruth knocked in fifty-four home runs that year, six under the mark he had set the season before which endured for more than a half century. The English Channel was full of swimmers after Gertrude Ederle, a young mother, had shown them the way. It was an age of sensation, of scandal, of depravity and of nonsense. The Hall-Mills murder case was the biggest Roman holiday of the decade. Tommy Manville, heir to an asbestos fortune, was marrying young girls and leaving them after a few months with million-dollar settlements. Al Capone in Chicago and Dutch Schultz in New York were making headlines with their murderous exploits, and a man named Alvin "Shipwreck" Kelly sat atop a flagpole for twenty-three days, claiming the world championship.

When Shirley was six months old, George and Gertrude, both Republicans, went to the polls to vote for Herbert Hoover, who was elected in a landslide. One year later George told his wife he hated to go to work. No matter how early he arrived at the branch on Sixteenth Street and Vermont, depositors were already lined up two and three deep at the doors to the California Bank, waiting to withdraw their savings.

The bubble had burst; the deepest economic depression in history had struck. Banks and businesses were failing; each month hundreds of people were leaping from high windows, cutting their throats and shooting themselves as their fortunes evaporated; uncounted numbers were being saved from starvation by soup kitchens as factories and shops shut their doors.

From the best of times it had become the worst. Paradoxically, those bleak days, so filled with despair for America and the world, were in large measure responsible for the enormous success of the little girl toddling around the house in Santa Monica.

The Depression did not spare the Temples. George was laid off for a while when the bank closed, but was rehired a short time afterward when it reopened. Three times the bank shut down and opened, causing shivers of worry to the family. Though it finally remained open, the entire staff took heavy cuts in salary. Money to support his family with its growing needs, not to mention appetites, was consequently scarce.

Still, Gertrude insisted on putting some aside for dancing lessons for Shirley. In September of 1931, when Shirley was almost four, Gertrude enrolled her at Meglin, a professional institution staffed by present and former stage and movie people. It taught youngsters a broad range of show-business skills from acrobatics to tap and ballet as well as acting and singing. Some pupils were sent there to sharpen their social graces, but for most there was a clear objective: to get into films or on the stage. Gertrude learned to drive so that she would be able to take Shirley for her lessons.

The school was founded by Mrs. Ethel Meglin, a dancing teacher from Cincinnati who had arrived in California in the early 1920s with her husband. She rented a vacant building on the old Mack Sennett lot and opened a dance studio for children, beginning with thirty pupils, all of them eager for stage and movie careers. Shirley Temple and Judy Garland are Meglin's most famous alumnae. Judy and her two sisters, Virginia and Jane, studied singing, dancing and acrobatics, with their mother, Mrs. Ethel Gumm, playing the piano in exchange for their lessons.

Ethel Meglin managed to book her charges into the Loew's State Theatre in Los Angeles in a revue produced by Fanchon and

Marco, which billed the troupe as the "The Famous Meglin Kiddies."

The act gave Ethel Meglin a gigantic start: within a few years her "wonder kiddies" had earned her a fortune and she was franchising school after school all across the country. Eventually there were forty of them offering professional lessons to more than ten thousand young pupils. It was the largest and most important school of its kind, known to all movie companies, a fact which drew mothers with stage ambitions for their children to its door. Shrewdly, Ethel Meglin devised a short training course for the mothers too, offering advice on what to say and how to act and present their children when answering advertisements for casting.

Shirley impressed her teacher, who told Gertrude she was "a truly remarkable child." Dressed in the short simple blue costume which the school required of its students, she surprised the instructor by picking up dance steps accurately and rapidly.

In the spring of 1932, a few months after her enrollment, a director named Charles Lamont received a telegram from his boss in New York. He was told to "get some children" and have them at the studio two weeks hence. The man who sent the message was Earle Woolridge Hammons, a movie pioneer who figured prominently in Shirley's career and helped launch Bob Hope, Bing Crosby, Danny Kaye and other celebrated figures and has been given insufficient credit for his many innovations. Short films were one.

In addition to Hope, Crosby and Kaye, Hammons made several early comedies with Buster Keaton, Larry Semon, Billy Gilbert, Pat Rooney and Edward Everett Horton, all of whom made indelible marks soon after. The roster of writing talent which created their stories and devised their antics was a Who's Who of future literary greats, including Eugene O'Neill, Edna Ferber, Rex Beach, Faith Baldwin and Zane Grey.

By the early 1930s, after sound films had arrived, Hammons discovered that one of his more popular series starring children, called Big Boy, was in trouble. The recording equipment of the early talkies could register only voices with a frequency of fifteen thousand vibrations per second, and a child's tones were rarely loud enough to reach this level. Hammons spun off another thought: He would continue and even expand his children's series, but he would have the youngsters mouth their lines and would dub in the deeper and louder voices of adult actors.

A message was dispatched to Lamont, and Hammons boarded the *Twentieth Century Limited* for Los Angeles. Lamont called an assistant and told him to call Meglin. "Tell them to get their kids ready," he said. "I'll be out next week." The assistant called the manager at Meglin, who tacked a notice on the bulletin board.

The arrival of a movie representative never failed to create high excitement. The obligatory blue dance uniforms were left home that day and every young girl was dressed to the nines in finery calculated to catch the eye. An hour ahead of time, several dozen little princesses in pastels, lace and big bows were lined up alongside almost as many boys in velvet short pants and ruffled shirts.

Somehow Gertrude had failed to see the notice. She arrived at the school for Shirley's regular class and was surprised to see the crowd of children in their fancy clothes.

"What is it," she asked a teacher, "a party?"

"Oh no," the teacher explained. "It's an interview. A movie director is looking for screen children. Why don't you bring Shirley in?"

Gertrude glanced down at her daughter, who was wearing her dance costume. "Not looking like that," she said firmly. "All those children are dressed up."

"Oh, bring her along," the teacher urged Gertrude, explaining that no pictures would be taken. The director, she said, would "just look at the children and ask them questions."

Lamont and an aide drove up, and the mothers were asked to leave. The director spoke briefly to each child and watched closely as each walked the length of the room and back.

That was all. Shirley came out and took her mother's hand. On the drive home, she revealed little to Gertrude about what had transpired. Later Gertrude learned that Shirley had hidden under the piano until induced to come out and audition.

Three days later, the phone rang. It was Lamont's assistant.

Would she bring her daughter down to Educational's studios for a screen test?

She would and she did, joining dozens of other parents and youngsters who had received a similar summons.

Recalling that day in an interview for the Columbia University Oral History Project, Earle Hammons said, "I was walking across the grounds of the studio talking to Charlie. A lot of kids were waiting. One little child caught my coat and pulled it a little bit and I looked down and saw the most beautiful little thing, and I picked her up in my arms and I said, 'What's your name?'

"She said, 'Shirley.'

"I said, 'What are you doing here?'

"'I'm going to work for you,' she answered.

"So I told Charlie, 'You want to watch her. She knows what she wants.'"

3

Princess of Poverty Row

Just after New Year's Day of 1932, Gertrude drove Shirley, fresh and dainty in a pink dress, a matching bow in her hair, to Gower Street and Santa Monica Boulevard, a part of Hollywood scornfully termed Poverty Row.

Gower was not a people slum but a thoroughfare along which were nondescript, mostly wooden buildings housing the fringe movie companies which were sprouting up like mushrooms after a spring rain. Dozens of little enterprises, begun on large hopes but little money, went into business each year and went right out again, leaving behind pieces of scenery, broken equipment, unpaid rent and, worst of all, angry, unpaid actors. Nearly all of the companies have been swept into oblivion and forgotten. Gary Cooper and Clark Gable broke into pictures as riders for Westerns churned out on the Row.

And Shirley Temple began here.

Educational was one of the sturdiest of the infant companies spawned by the movie industry; its grosses reached $14 million a year before it too disappeared. These studios turned out instant movies, few of which took more than a week to make, most requiring only a few days, and expenditures were deliberately kept very low. Compared to the others, Hammons was a spendthrift. His one-reelers cost $10,000, two-reelers $20,000, and, while other companies paid their actors from $5 to $1.50 a day, he paid $10.

The Gower Street studios bordered on open fields and vacant lots; when a company took its actors and crew outside its back door, it was "on location." With the addition of strategically placed painted scenery, the open land was converted into a range for cowboys, a lush African jungle, an idyllic country setting or anything else in the script.

Inside Educational's barnlike studio, Gertrude and Shirley joined dozens of other parents and children who had received similar calls. Their babble subsided when Lamont entered and mounted a chair to address them. It rose to a crescendo again when the director made it clear he wasn't interested in the fancy garments the mothers had put on their kids.

"Take off their clothes," he ordered. "On that side"—pointing—"you'll find a bunch of diapers. Put them on your children and attach them with those safety pins." The pins were six inches long.

Howls of dismay came from many of the children who protested, justifiably enough, that they had outgrown diapers and had no intention of returning to them. A number, particularly boys, argued so vociferously that their mothers reluctantly took them home. Shirley, however, had no qualms about the costume. "She would have worn diapers, evening gowns or nothing with complete indifference," Gertrude said. Nonetheless, she confessed she held her breath when her daughter, diapered and with the huge pin stuck horizontally across her middle, marched in front of the camera.

She was not chosen for a part. Jack Hays, producer of the planned series, picked a pretty little girl named Audrey Leonard to be his leading lady and told her mother to have her report in three days. "How wayward the decrees of Fate are," Thackeray wrote in *Vanitas Vanitatum*. Audrey fell ill. Hays, calling down maledictions on his own fate, looked about for another child.

His wife remembered Shirley and reminded her husband of her.

Hays called the Temple home and asked Gertrude to bring her daughter to the studio to go to work.

Hammons' notion was to film a series of shorts called Baby Burlesks which would satirize the current hit movies, using preschool children in the roles grownups were playing. The tots would be cowboys and Indians, cannibals and missionaries, vamps and chorus girls, boxers and their handlers, soldiers and their women. They would be costumed in basic diaper, adorned with accouterments of their characters: gun belts for the plainsmen, overseas caps for doughboys, top hats for men-about-town.

Shirley's first screen role was in a nine-minute film called *War Babies*, a take-off on *What Price Glory?*, the classic antiwar play written eight years earlier by Maxwell Anderson and Laurence Stallings and later made into a movie starring Victor McLaglen and Edmund Lowe. Shirley, as Charmaine, the French girl over whom the rambunctious Captain Flagg and Sergeant Quirt battled, wore an off-the-shoulder peasant blouse, a garter below the right knee and a rose in her hair as she flirted with tot-sized soldiers at a milk bar. The first thing she said in a movie was a French phrase she didn't understand: *"Mais oui, mon cher."*

Her next picture was *The Runt Page*, a ten-minute burlesque of the Ben Hecht–Charles MacArthur play about Chicago newspaper reporters, *The Front Page*, which had been made into the first of its several movie incarnations. Shirley was "Lulu Parsnips," a character spoofing Louella O. Parsons, the Hollywood columnist. She played opposite "Raymond Bunions," who was supposed to represent the newsman Damon Runyon. (The film was never released to movie theaters. It remained on the shelf until almost two decades later, when it was discovered and shown on television.)

That year and in the early months of 1933, Shirley acted in eight films of the Burlesk series, which grew rapidly in popularity. In advertisements aimed at exhibitors in movie trade journals, she was listed as the "star." The whole lot of them were in dreadful taste, most offensive by any standards; perhaps worse, they exposed Shirley and all the other children to possible serious physical injury.

37

In one movie, Shirley portrayed Morelegs Sweetrick, a less than thinly veiled version of Marlene Dietrich. Done up in a short, tight sequined gown, she was told to place a bare leg atop a hassock in the sexy pose made famous by the German actress in *The Blue Angel*. A poster of Shirley in that posture was distributed to theaters. *Polly-Tix in Washington,* billed as a political satire, was worse. Here Shirley, costumed in a bra and panties of black lace, played the role of a capital coquette. The advertising matter sent to the exhibitors carries its own commentary:

> *Polly-Tix in Washington* is a political satire set to music. The kids play the politicians.
> Shirley plays the role of Polly, she vamps her way into the life of a mighty important man in Washington. Will she lead him astray or will he have some effect on her and make her mend her ways?

The risks which the youngsters were required to take would scarcely be sanctioned by modern state laws governing child actors. In one scene, the story called for Shirley to be taken for a wild ride in a carriage drawn by an ostrich. To get the effect they wanted, the directors devised the idea of putting a blindfold on the ostrich and then, when the camera began to roll, removing it and letting him go free. However, the moment its eyes were covered, the bird became nervous. When the bandage was pulled away he bolted forward, terrifying—and endangering—Shirley until he was stopped.

In *Kid'n' Africa,* a lampoon of the Tarzan-Jane pictures, she was saved from cannibals by a tot swinging from a vine. Nearly fifty years later, the recollections of a horrifying scene she was made to perform was still with her.

"I was Jane to a little boy who was Tarzan," she said, "and we had to run through a jungle. I was being chased by little black boys who were playing the African natives. What they did in that, they wanted all the children to fall at one time. Jane, or Shirley, got through on the path, and then they put a wire up and tripped all the little black boys at once and, of course, they all fell in a heap and some of their legs were cut, and this was something I thought was terrible." The injured children burst into tears, Shirley along with them even though she herself had not been hurt.

Today's psychologically oriented mothers might express shock at the kinds of roles Shirley was playing, but movie audiences of the thirties were delighted and Gertrude does not seem to have protested. In none of the many subsequent interviews she gave did she voice anything but praise and gratitude for the start her daughter was given.

She and George went to a local theater to see Shirley in her first movie, and her account two years later in *America* magazine read:

> We invited all our friends, and they crowded the theater with enthusiasm. The picture lasted ten minutes. Shirley merely flitted across the screen a few times and said only two lines. But my head swam and the goose flesh popped out on my arms. I think I cried a little. George squeezed my hand. Oh well, we were proud. It was just our little girl doing something wonderful, like saying her first words, and we were happy.

George's happiness as Shirley's career moved forward with Educational doubtless stemmed from a more practical reason. Shirley was earning ten dollars a day, forty dollars for working four days a week. Diana Serra Cary, who as Baby Peggy was a silent screen star in the early 1920s, asserts, "By then, Mr. Temple's bank was on the verge of being closed and Shirley's forty dollars was no laughing matter."

Inevitably, Shirley grew and began looking somewhat absurd in diapers. She was less and less, then not at all, in the series. She was cast in a number of other Educational shorts and was raised to fifteen dollars a day. Came the time, however, when those too closed. So did the money.

The Temples had signed an agreement with Hays, the supervisor of the shorts, granting him an option on Shirley's services. He made the rounds of the other studios and, urged on by Gertrude, got Shirley some parts. She had a walk-on engagement in a two-reeler for Paramount starring curly-haired, boyish Charles "Buddy" Rogers, who became a screen idol, and a bit part in something called *The Red-Haired Alibi.*

Gertrude kept after Hays. One day, seeking work for Shirley, he approached a friend he had met on the Row, thirty-six-year-old Henry Hathaway, who, as an assistant director, had helped grind out a dozen or more Westerns. A child actor himself at the age of nine, Hathaway had literally grown up in the movies. He was a close friend of Gary Cooper, whom he was to direct in a number of films, including the legendary *Lives of a Bengal Lancer* and *Peter Ibbetson*. (Cooper would remember Shirley all his life. An unparalleled scene-stealer himself, he was outclassed by Shirley when Hathaway hired her to play with him.)

Hathaway, now eighty-three and only recently retired, is still the blend of kindness and crustiness actors had known over the years. In his Bel-Air home, he recalls the time he hired Shirley for her first major movie.

Henry Hathaway: "This fellow [Jack Hays] came to me and said, 'Henry, I have this kid under contract and her mother wouldn't let me off the hook. She's getting too big to play these kids in diapers. Do you think you can find something for her?'

"I said, 'Sure, let's take a look at her.' So he sent her over and when I saw her, this little doll, I grabbed her right away. I had a Western under production then, a Zane Grey film called *To the Last Man*, for Paramount, with a lot of good actors—Randolph Scott, Gail Patrick, Esther Ralston, Buster Crabbe, Jack LaRue, Noah Beery, Barton MacLane.

"I saw in that child a little miracle. She was bright, inventive and charming, rare for a youngster that age. I used her then because I thought she was great, and I continued to use her for that reason. She was only five, yet she had a magic you couldn't define. If you can find out what it was, if you can explain it, you're better than I am. I spent my whole life in this business and I'll be damned if I can."

Shirley may have been bright and inventive, but she was also a little foolhardy. Hathaway could not recall any other actress who fought back against a mule.

Hathaway: "One of the scenes called for Shirley to be playing herself at a little table in a barn, having a tea party. Close by, we had a mule. As Shirley, following the script, poured tea for herself and a pretended guest, the mule wandered over, attracted by the sugar the prop man had placed on the table, and began to lick at it.

"Now, this wasn't in the script. Shirley was irritated and tried to shoo him away. I ordered the camera to keep going, because this began to look good. The mule refused to move and kept on eating the sugar. At this point, Shirley got up from the table and, with her two small hands, tried to push him out of the way.

"This got the mule irritated. He turned around, and with his two back legs he hauled off at her with a kick. She ducked back and he missed, but instead of stopping or running away, and before we could rush in and grab her away, she strode over and kicked the mule right back. She gave him one hell of a boot in the ass. This surprised the mule, who ran away. Shirley, completely composed, returned to her table, sat down and resumed her scene. We got it all on film."

While she waited for her scenes, Shirley wandered about the set, cool and poised, surprising the cast by her precocity. "Once I saw her sitting on a low truck," Hathaway said, "the kind we use to move furniture, looking uncomfortable. 'Is anything wrong?' I asked her. She answered, 'You know, the ventilation here isn't very good. Not that it's hot and sultry, it's just the ventilation.' Now, where in the world did she learn to talk like that? She hadn't even been to school yet."

To the Last Man came and went unheralded, and Shirley with it. Gertrude, disenchanted with Hays, visited one casting office after another, sometimes with Shirley in tow, sometimes alone, with the required photographs and list of credits. There were a few jobs, in minor pictures: an unbilled part as the child of a sharecropper in *Carolina*, which starred Janet Gaynor and Lionel Barrymore; a walk-through appearance aboard a jungle steamer in *Mandalay*, with Kay Francis and Ricardo Cortez.

Gertrude was disheartened. The family was being pinched with increasing severity in that desperate year for the country. The Temples heard on the radio that many middle-class people like them

41

were reduced to begging on the street, that two million hungry Americans had taken to the road as wandering vagabonds and that shanty towns, or "Hoovervilles," were springing up in every city. They went to bed each night frightened, wondering what lay ahead if George's bank should close. For months, Gertrude received no offers for Shirley except from Harpo Marx, who saw her one day at the Paramount studios while she was filming *New Deal Rhythm* and was enchanted. Marx, who was childless, reportedly told Gertrude he would pay her fifty thousand dollars if she would agree to let him adopt Shirley. The offer was rejected.

Then, on a summer afternoon, with nothing to do and little in sight, Gertrude drove to Wilshire Boulevard in Beverly Hills with Shirley to spend a few hours at a movie. In one of those coincidences that occur more frequently in films than in life, they met a stocky dark-haired pipe-smoking man, and the encounter, quite literally, changed their lives.

4

A Talk with Her Discoverer

A number of people helped boost Shirley Temple to her stardom—we have met Hammons, who is surely one, and Lamont, who has a claim—but Shirley herself has tagged Jay Gorney, now eighty-five, as the one most responsible.

On the wall of his West End Avenue apartment in New York City is a photograph of her with the inscription "To Jay Gorney who discovered me in the Fox Wilshire Theatre." It is signed by Shirley and her mother.

In 1968, Sondra Gorney, Jay's second wife, was at the Minneapolis airport to meet Shirley, who was flying in from San Francisco to address the annual conference of the National Multiple Sclerosis Society. Shirley was a member of the organization's national board, and Mrs. Gorney was publicity coordinator for the session.

Inside the terminal, Mrs. Gorney introduced herself, and Shirley, married by then to Charles Black, looked surprised. "Are you related to Jay Gorney?" she asked.

"I'm his wife," Sondra replied.

Shirley's face lit up. "That dear man!" she said. "How is he? I didn't know he was still alive. Why, he discovered me!"

Gorney, who was brought up in Detroit, earned a law degree

43

from the University of Michigan, then put his diploma into a bureau drawer and began doing what he loved best—writing songs. Settling in New York, he haunted Tin Pan Alley and soon became successful. He wrote songs for Shubert shows, *Earl Carroll's Sketch Book* and the *Ziegfeld Follies*. In 1932, he composed the music for the lyrics of E. Y. "Yip" Harburg for the number that became virtually the theme song of the Depression, "Brother, Can You Spare a Dime?"

A year later he joined the westward migration to Hollywood, where the era of the big musical was getting underway. In 1933, *42nd Street*, with Warner Baxter, Bebe Daniels, Dick Powell and the then-unknown Ruby Keeler, had captivated the country, and, in the movie capital's tradition—which still persists— of imitating a good thing in hopes of mining the same gold, more of the same genre were being budgeted by the studios.

The Fox Film Company had one in the hopper, too, a musical called *Fox Movietone Revue* for which Will Rogers, the cowboy philosopher, had supplied the story ideas with Philip Klein and Lew Brown and had written the screenplay. Brown, who had just broken up with his fellow songwriters Buddy DeSylva and Ray Henderson, needed a new collaborator. He sought out Jay, who shrugged and said, "Why not?"

Gorney went to work on the musical, which was soon retitled *Stand Up and Cheer*. Baxter, riding high after his tremendous success in *42nd Street*, had been signed to star with Madge Evans, and in the cast were James Dunn, John Boles, Ralph Morgan and Tess Gardella (Aunt Jemima).

The scenario is about a producer who is summoned to Washington to head up a newly created department as Secretary of Amusements, in which post he sends teams of entertainers around the nation to bring smiles to the people and cause them to forget the Depression and its woes. Toward the end, James Dunn would sing "Baby Take a Bow," and then through his legs "Baby" would appear, a small girl who would sing new words, "Daddy, take a bow."

For days, a search was conducted to find a child for the role.

Jay Gorney: "Winfield Sheehan, the Fox chief of production, told

44

Lew and me that he had just the right one, a prize package he was waiting to show us. He led us to a stage and there was this little girl, whose name I blessedly have forgotten, and he said, 'Sing for us, dear.'

"Well, the little girl started to talk first. She was doing Mae West imitations. 'Come up'n see me sometime'—that kind of thing. It embarrassed me to see an eight-year-old girl go through those gyrations and sing a song with movements I didn't particularly like. But who dares speak against the vice-president in charge of production?

"I'd been working long hours at the studio and I guess I was a little brain-weary. I decided to go to a movie to clear my mind. There was a theater only about five or six blocks from the studio which was showing a picture I had wanted to see, now long since forgotten, so my wife and I went there in the afternoon. I guess it was about two o'clock or so.

"When I walked into the lobby to buy my tickets, I saw a little girl with reddish-gold ringlets who was looking at the photographs of coming attractions in glass frames along the walls. She was humming and singing to herself, very unself-consciously, and doing a few dance steps.

"I stopped and said to my wife, 'Have you ever seen a cuter child?'

"'She's adorable,' she said.

"I looked around to see who was accompanying her, but saw nobody. Well, I don't usually talk to strange little girls, but this one was just charming, so I went up to her.

"'Hello,' I said. 'What's your name?'

"'Shirley.'

"'What's your last name?'

"'Temple.'

"'Where did you learn to dance?'

"'I go to school.'

"'Are you here alone?' I asked.

"'My mommy's over there.' I saw a tall attractive woman a few feet away. I went over to her and said I had been talking to that little girl (pointing to Shirley) and she said you are her mommy. 'I am,' she said.

"'Has she ever been in the theater or done anything in pictures?' I asked.

"The woman explained that her daughter had been in a number of shorts but nothing more.

"'Would she like to be in a major film?' I asked.

"'I think so. Certainly, certainly.'

"'Cer'nly would,' Shirley chimed in.

"The mother was a charming woman and she did seem very eager. So I asked her to bring Shirley to my office at the studio the following day. She asked what time, I told her two o'clock. She said she would have her there.

"You promise?"

"'I promise.'

"I went back to Shirley, who was still looking at the pictures.

"Your mommy said she will come to my office at the studio and you will come with her," I said.

"She gave me a big smile.

"The next day I waited. No Shirley Temple, no Mrs. Temple. I asked the doorman if anybody had come to see me. No, he told me, nobody had.

"Finally, one night at my home in Beverly Hills, I got a telephone call. It was Mrs. Temple. She said, 'Mr. Gorney, we've been coming to the studio every day, to your lot, and they tell us there's no such name as Gorney.'

"Well, I found out that the studio directory changes every month. I had arrived there on the second, so my name would not normally appear until the following month. I asked the guards and they told me, 'You're new here and we can't put your name on the list of people who work here until you're recognized as belonging here. But if you insist on getting this girl in, I'll put your name on the list and she can come in tomorrow.

"Mrs. Temple finally did show up, and I must say, if it wasn't for her astuteness and drive, that little thing might have been lost to the world. Her mother was a sweet woman, not a stage mother at all.

"I had a little cottage on the lot, with a big grand piano and all the things I needed to compose my music. The doorbell rang, I opened it and there stood mother and daughter. 'We haven't got much time,' I told them. 'I want Shirley to learn this song quickly.'

"I went to the piano, hoisted Shirley on top and ran through the words just twice. Well, she amazed me. She sang it through perfectly. She was cute as could be. I asked her, 'Can you dance to that rhythm?' She said she could, so I told her to stand on the piano and I played a little introduction, ta-da, ta dum-dum-dum, and she went into a tap routine for two choruses.

"It was exactly what I had hoped for. I went to the phone and called Mr. Sheehan. 'I've got a little girl, just the type we're looking for. I'd like you to see her. She's in my bungalow now.'

"He said, 'Mr. Gorney, anybody wants to see me comes to my office.'

"I explained that I needed a piano to show him what she could do, and none was available in his office. He replied that he was too busy to go see anyone.

"I said, 'Mr. Sheehan, I know that, and I apologize, but this is something I can't show you unless you come to my bungalow. If you will do so I don't think you'll be disappointed.'

"He said, 'Gorney, you attend to the music. I'll attend to the casting.'

"I said, 'I'll do that, Mr. Sheehan, but you're losing something that's quite wonderful. What can you lose? Come on over.'

"He said, 'All right, but it better be good.'

"I hung up and began rehearsing Shirley some more. As we were going through the number again, the door to my cottage opened and Mr. Sheehan came in. Shirley, still on top of the piano, did it for him.

"'I think she'll make it,' he said when she finished.

"'Mr. Sheehan,' I told him, 'I'm sure she'll make it.'"

Two weeks later, Harold Lloyd wandered into the cavernous recording studio on the Fox lot and stood at the back, next to an anxious Gertrude, saying nothing. Shirley, who had just been awakened from a fifteen-minute nap, was led to the cylindrical microphone and looked up at it helplessly until an assistant director found a table for her to stand on. Then, with a full orchestra behind her and an audience of dozens of showgirls in spangled tights, she sang her song.

When she finished, the great bespectacled comedian said, half to himself, half to Gertrude, "My God! Another Coogan!"

Until Shirley came along, Jackie Coogan had been the most famous child star the movies had ever produced. He was, in fact, the first, for while the wildly popular Mary Pickford, in petticoats and ringlets, played preteen roles, she was well into her maturity before she could leave them behind. To be mentioned on the same level as Coogan by a professional of Lloyd's stature was praise indeed.

Coogan had fed First National for several years, ever since 1920, when he became an international idol for his winsome performance in *The Kid* with Charlie Chaplin. When Shirley appeared, the search for "another Coogan" who would pull them into the movie houses with the same powerful suction was becoming frenetic. Her swift ascent assured the rise of so many other moppets that the next two decades were to become enshrined as the golden era of child stars, never again to be duplicated.

Jane Withers, Judy Garland and Deanna Durbin rose with her; the fresh-faced, wholesome Deanna kept Universal Pictures solvent. Mickey Rooney, Bobby Breen, Bonita Granville and Freddie Bartholomew were part of the golden age, followed in the forties by Elizabeth Taylor, Margaret O'Brien, Peggy Ann Garner and Natalie Wood. They all made money. As the children's era began moving into high gear, the studio that produced most of Shirley's movies actually signed up the Dionne quintuplets, who had become world curiosities following their birth in 1934. They appeared in three films, including one called *Five of a Kind*, but all three were failures, prompting Frances Marion, the screenwriter, to observe that "it was obviously straining the formula."

When Fox executives viewed the rushes of Shirley's song and dance in *Stand Up and Cheer*, they heard the jingle of cash registers in movie ticket booths. She made a hit, a big one. At one point, Jimmy Dunn fluffed a line; Shirley stopped and scolded him. She told him what he ought to have said and done. The cameras, turning, recorded the incident. The executives howled. "Let it stay in," said one. "Rewrite the script!" It was done; the scene remained in the picture and is still there on late-night television.

For the preview, held in an outlying theater, Shirley wore a brand-new dress. Gertrude, saying she was too young to go at night with all the movie executives, took her to a matinee. Just before they were to leave the house, Shirley did what one can reasonably assume hundreds of other young children inevitably do. She accidentally locked herself in the bathroom. George was at work, the boys were at school, so Gertrude, with the help of a woman neighbor, hoisted a ladder to the window and got her out. They barely made it to the theater on time.

That night, after another showing, the audience applauded Shirley spontaneously and Sheehan yelled exultantly, "She's stolen the picture!" *Variety* did not argue with that assessment, reporting that Shirley was "the unofficial star of this Fox musical." *The New York Times,* in the first review of a Temple performance, called her "a delightful child," and even *Commonweal* wrote that she was "vastly ingratiating in spite of being pictured as one of the most absurdly spoiled imps of the American home."

Winfield Sheehan offered Gertrude a seven-year contract at $150 a week for her daughter's services. Coming at that low ebb in their fortunes, the money was mind-reeling, but now Gertrude began to have second thoughts about the long-range consequences of a screen career.

That evening, she and George were up most of the night, balancing the advantages against the evils. As dawn broke, they were still undecided. Two more days passed before they reached their decision: Yes, provided the contract contained a clause—the first of its kind in those years—that the parents of the actress could declare it null and void if, in their sole discretion, they felt that Shirley's movie work was harming her personality or preventing her from growing up in a normal manner as a normal child.

They presented their views to Sheehan, who agreed. The clause was never invoked, although the life that was now beginning to unfold was anything but "normal." It was a fantasy that could scarcely be imagined.

Sheehan, the former Buffalo police reporter who was now in charge of her life, brought her along slowly, nurturing her like a rare camellia. Concerned that other actors and staff members on the lot would fawn over, coddle and thereby spoil her, he issued orders that she must not eat at the studio commissary, but alone in her dressing room with her mother. His intention was to keep her innocence and genuineness intact, but it was the beginning of an isolation for Shirley that would intensify as time went on.

Sheehan put her in small roles: the daughter of gambler Arnold Rothstein, played by Spencer Tracy, in a film called *Now I'll Tell*, and a few lines in the movie of Kathleen Norris' novel *Change of Heart*, which starred the still-remembered lovers of *Seventh Heaven*, Janet Gaynor and Charles Farrell.

On loan to Paramount, she was cast as the child in *Little Miss Marker* who is left as security with a racetrack bookie for a twenty-dollar loan by her gambler father. Based on a story by Damon Runyon, it was a perfect vehicle with which to ride to stardom. William Boehnel wrote in the *New York World-Telegram*, "The child is absolutely irresistible." *Variety* said that women would "gush over the youngster," and *The New York Times* threw its hat into the air. "Little Shirley Temple," wrote Mordaunt Hall, "the lovely tiny lass of *Stand Up and Cheer*, is virtually the stellar performer in the present work and no more engaging child has been beheld on the screen."

The Temple meteor was on the rise.

5

"Sparkle, Shirley, sparkle!"

By the fall of 1934, after only two major films, Shirley's pictures had already given Fox Films a badly needed infusion of money and saved Winfield Sheehan's job. Studio executives had been about to sack him when they learned of an astute financial deal he had made, at Shirley's expense. Not unheard-of in Hollywood then and now, he was paying her little and lending her out for a lot: her salary was $150 a week, the loan fee $1,000. For this, he got himself a new one-year contract calling for $1,000 a day.

Still, he lasted only that one year. In 1935, Fox and Twentieth Century arranged their historic merger. Sheehan faded into oblivion, and Shirley's career was placed in the hands of Darryl F. Zanuck, an authentic movie mogul/eccentric. The thirty-one-year-old Zanuck, a short and stocky man, installed himself in an office the size of a small ballroom, sat behind a huge desk and carried a cut-down polo mallet which he constantly rapped against the high boots he wore. He generally ate two breakfasts, one at home and the second at the office with his executives, often followed by a pair of lunches.

He terrified everybody, except the little fireball he now had in his company, Shirley Temple. Trusting nobody, Zanuck would slip silently into the various sets on the lot to see what was going on; he called it observing, but the cast and crew, including Shirley, termed it spying. He would position himself behind a partition and stick his neck out while he looked. Shirley, eagle-eyed, often caught him. She would run to the director and whisper, "The spy is here."

One day, on such an expedition, Zanuck spotted Shirley—who had not noticed him this time—tip-toeing behind a wall and poking her head out, exactly as he did. Then she emerged and walked about the set in a remarkably accurate imitation of the studio boss. Said Allan Dwan, one of Shirley's directors, who recalled the story, "Zanuck didn't like it one bit, but he said nothing. Shirley was too valuable."

All of her important films, the ones that catapulted her to fame and are still shown on television, were made between 1934 and the close of the decade. From June to December of 1934 alone, she starred in three. Eight others were filmed in the next two years, two in 1937, three in 1938 and two more in 1939.

That they were cranked out like sausages and were not of uniform quality made little difference. They were all hits. Each was produced at a cost ranging from $150,000 to $300,000, and each grossed between $1 million and $1.5 million. By 1935, when she was seven years old and a star for just one year, she became the country's champion box-office draw.

Through all of her child stardom years, Gertrude Temple "monitored Shirley's entire existence," in Sidney Skolsky's phrase. Skolsky, the Hollywood correspondent who arrived in Los Angeles at the start of the Temple phenomenon, was impressed by the scope and extent of Mama Temple's contribution. "She looked after everything," he said, "leaving nothing out." Allan Dwan asserted, "The little girl was the instrument on which her mother played." And David Butler, who directed Shirley in four films, agrees with them all; "Gertrude," he says, "had a firm hold on her all the time."

Gertrude negotiated all of the contracts, engaging attorney Loyd Wright to advise her and nail down the provisions legally. In the beginning, she included a clause calling for $150 a week for her own services, in addition to Shirley's salary of $1,000. By 1935, she asked for and got $4,000 for Shirley and $500 for herself. She also insisted upon, and was granted, a $20,000 bonus for Shirley to be paid at the conclusion of every film. And by the end of the decade, Gertrude's remuneration had gone up to $1,000 a week.

At home, Gertrude ran a tight ship; her guide word in Shirley's twig-bending years was discipline, stern, strong and unyielding. She let her daughter know from the very beginning that "I wouldn't stand for any funny business." She never, in her words, "coddled or babied" her, nor gave her any more attention than she felt was needed or warranted. "I never allowed her to be rocked or petted too much," she said, "even as an infant."

Gertrude tolerated no disobedience. "If she ever offered to rebel against my wishes," she said, "I would use force to see that she did what she was told. I have spanked her soundly upon three or four occasions when she was slow about minding me, but I do not find it necessary to use force often." Gertrude was aware that many psychologists of her time frowned on corporal punishment as a means of making children behave, but she countered with what she felt was the bottom line: "It works."

Gertrude believed that children should be given chores even at early ages even though they do not carry them out any too well, because performing a function instilled a sense of responsibility and built self-reliance. So Shirley helped clear the table after dinner almost as soon as she was able to walk. Shirley's prideful recollection is that she did it rather well, though one time, in a frisky mood, she began what she called a "spring dance," in the midst of which her foot slipped. She fell and gashed her lip. Bleeding profusely, she was rushed by ambulance to the hospital, where she was stitched up.

Shirley, then, was a "good" child—most of the time. Gertrude said that she never did any of the things that drive other mothers up the wall: she did not track in mud, smash her toys, smear the walls with paints and crayons, talk back to her parents or throw temper tantrums. She marched off when told to be bathed by George in the evening, a practice begun early and continued until she was seven, and she ate what was put before her. Gertrude prepared the right things. For breakfast, there was orange juice or half a grapefruit, hot cereal, a single coddled egg and milk. Lunch was a sandwich, fruit and milk. For dinner she served chicken, fish, salad, fruit and vegetables. Shirley didn't even balk at eating spinach. Bedtime was eight-thirty, on the dot. She wasn't even sick, except for five or six colds.

Still, she had her moments. She squabbled with her brother Sonny, mostly about a pet Scotty. She would interrupt him when he was busy doing schoolwork, causing the kind of uproar familiar in many households. Once, she and Sonny wanted to play the piano at the same time. Sonny, unimpressed by her star status, pushed her off the stool; Shirley, claiming she had been there first, erupted. They almost came to blows when Gertrude, hearing the commotion, rushed in and stopped the fracas.

Shirley was perky, though, and opinionated. At the dinner table, George, Gertrude and the boys would frequently become involved in a discussion on some current topic. Shirley, who would know practically nothing about the subject, would pipe up anyway, tell them all she thought they were wrong and proceed to explain why. Then Gertrude would put her in her place. "At the table," she once admitted, "I find it necessary to ask Shirley to be still, as she feels quite as big as the rest of us . . . and when we are deep in a discussion she is apt to say we are wrong and tells us why she thinks so. It is a habit I do not want her to get into . . . . I believe children should really be seen more than heard."

Gertrude never left Shirley's side during the making of all her hit movies. She was there for every take, and Shirley watched her mother to see if she was performing well. Recognizing this mother–daughter interaction, Allan Dwan used Gertrude as a conduit for his orders. "The mother," he said, "was very alert and would listen to all the instructions that were given. Absentmindedly, I would tell Shirley something I wanted her to do, and she would say, 'Yes, sir,' and hurry away. If she didn't go over to her mother, who would repeat to her what was to be done and take her off to a corner and rehearse her a little bit, she wouldn't do it right. She would do it her own way or whatever she made up, and so we were constantly having the mother come up and convey to her what we wanted. You knew better than to go up to Shirley and say, 'Hello, we're going to work together. Isn't that nice?' You didn't talk to her that way. You talked to her mother."

Dwan believed that Gertrude's ability to control Shirley at the studio was a direct consequence of the discipline at home. He said, "They bring them up that way—every order, everything they do, the way they dress, what the dress is, what part of the house she is allowed to do certain things in and not do certain things, what she is supposed to do when guests are in the house, either disappear or behave in a certain manner, come down and say good evening and leave. The mother had her strictly controlled at home, and so she could control her in the studio."

Mrs. Temple would allow no hairdresser to touch Shirley's honey-colored curls—that prohibition was written into the contracts. She would set each one at night, holding it in place with bobby pins, until it was brushed out in the morning. At the height of the Temple boom, a mini-debate broke out in the newspapers about the exact number of ringlets she had, fifty-four or fifty-six. Fan magazine writers appealed to Gertrude, who said fifty-six. She washed that famous head of hair every two weeks with castile soap and applied vinegar rinse to keep it from darkening.

Shirley came to be dependent upon her mother's presence on the set. When she was playing a scene, she would look out of a corner of an eye to see if Gertrude was there. Once Gertrude left for only thirty minutes without telling her daughter that she would be absent. When she returned, she found Shirley in tears and the entire company trying to console her.

On the set, Gertrude, powder puff in hand, would on occasion dash forward after a take to dust a too-shiny nose. If Shirley was not performing with sufficient emotion, she would take her aside and whisper to her like a baseball manager infusing a faltering pitcher with confidence.

Once, when she felt that Shirley was acting in a somewhat lackadaisical manner, she called out, "Sparkle, Shirley, sparkle!" Shirley instantly turned up her candlepower. In the rare instances when the director would not like the way she played a scene,

Gertrude would admonish her, "Come on, now. Play it like Shirley Temple would play it."

Before Shirley could read, Gertrude went over her lines with her in the evening at bedtime. She would try to explain the meaning of the next day's scenes and repeat the passages over and over. Even after Shirley learned to read, Gertrude continued to rehearse them with her. Shirley, who scored 155 on the Pintner-Cunningham intelligence test, which rates 135 and higher in the "genius" range, sopped up the lines with ease. Gertrude would hear her saying them in the bathroom and in the morning after she woke at seven. "This is not a task for Shirley," Gertrude said at the time, "although it sometimes is for me, since in a very subtle way I must communicate to her by my facial expression the feeling that goes with the lines. This necessitated my studying the entire script thoroughly."

In her early films Shirley probably did not understand the stories, the interplay of characters or even what was really going on inside the studio. Her acting, as Gertrude pointed out, was "really play," a game in which she was engaged, which she enjoyed and from which she learned a great deal.

Since the minds of normal children are more or less uncluttered slates, it is not unusual for them to possess excellent memories. Many parents are astonished at the way preschoolers can learn the story, even the exact words, read to them. Even so, Shirley's memory bordered on the phenomenal. After a few readings, she learned not only her own lines but everyone else's in the script, which caused some problems.

In *Now and Forever,* filmed late in 1934, she perplexed director Hathaway by stubbornly refusing to be put to bed in a scene with Carole Lombard. In the movie, Shirley had been deserted by her con-man father, played by Gary Cooper, and was being cared for by Lombard, his moll.

"The scene was simple," Hathaway said, "yet Shirley just would not allow herself to be placed in the bed. Finally, I stopped it and asked why she wouldn't do it. She told me, 'Mr. Hathaway, I go by the script. And it says that she pats me on my behind. And then I let her put me under the covers. I was waiting for her to do that, and she never did it.'

"That broke us all up. Lombard did the required patting, and Shirley slid docilely under the blanket."

Only once in anyone's memory did Shirley forget a line, and then it wasn't her own. Still, it caused a little trouble. In *Stowaway*, shot in 1936, she blew up in a scene with the noted Theatre Guild actress Helen Westley. Director William A. Seiter shot the sequence over and over, but Shirley stumbled every time. Everyone was astounded; Gertrude was nonplussed. Shirley began to cry.

Finally, after yet another fluff, Miss Westley suddenly clapped a hand to her brow and groaned loudly. "God forgive me," she said. "I left out a speech." It was a short one, but the omission had thrown Shirley off.

By the time she was ten, she had become more tolerant of actors' lapses. George Murphy, however, was wary when he appeared with her in *Little Miss Broadway*, having been forewarned by Warner Baxter, "Watch out for her. She'll drive you crazy!" He stuck closely to the lines except in one scene when he ad-libbed a big word and got away with it.

In the scene, Shirley, again an orphan, wants to enter a mansion but is told by the butler that nobody is home. Murphy, who actually lives there, tells her, "You can't trust that butler. He has hallucinations sometimes."

Later, Shirley asked, "What was that hallucin—something you said?"

"I just thought it sounded good," Murphy answered. "Did it bother you?"

"Oh no, Chief," she said airily. "Say anything you want as long as it makes sense."

6

The Best of Everything

By seven Shirley had her own dressing room, which was not a room at all but an entire little red-and-white house set down in a secluded part of the Fox lot. A white picket fence, painted weekly, enclosed a front yard where shrubs and a tree were planted, and a swing was installed for her. In the back was a henhouse and a bunny hutch where she played and bred bantam chickens and white rabbits. Every afternoon, on leaving, she would pick up a freshly laid egg and take it home for breakfast.

The bungalow had a large living room, furnished country style, and a tiny white piano. The bedroom, for napping, had cutouts of Mother Goose characters on the walls. There was also a bathroom with miniature-sized facilities, and a fully equipped kitchen, where Mrs. Temple cooked lunches which Shirley ate at a white enamel table. (The bungalow was so large that after Shirley retired it was turned into a studio dental clinic.) In addition to the bungalow, the studio provided her with a personal trailer which was pulled up next to the sound stage where she was working. She rested here between takes and changed costumes when it was not feasible to return to the bungalow. When she went on location, the trailer followed.

On February 27, 1935, Shirley won an Oscar, the first miniature Academy Award ever given to a child player. When she arrived at the Biltmore Hotel on South Olive Street, accompanied by her parents, she scared everybody by promptly getting lost.

The kidnapping and murder of the Lindbergh baby three years before was still fresh in everyone's mind, and the Temples had been receiving a series of extortion notes from a disturbed young man.

When Shirley was missed in the grand ballroom, studio executives joined actors, aides and the Temples in a frantic hunt, poking into alcoves, private suites and rest rooms. They found her outside, safe of course, posing in her brand-new pastel dress with pleated skirt and scalloped neckline for a photographer she knew. He had asked to take her picture, and, thinking he was acting under studio direction, she had gone with him. The award ceremony proceeded after the Temples calmed down, color returned to the movie tycoons' faces, and the photographer was summarily banished from Fox for one year.

Shirley presented the best-actress award to Claudette Colbert for *It Happened One Night*. When her own name was called, the rotund humorist Irvin S. Cobb, who was master of ceremonies, handed her a tiny gold-plated statuette, a special award by the Academy "in grateful recognition of her outstanding contribution to screen entertainment during the year 1934."

The following month, Shirley was asked to put her hand- and footprints into a block of cement under the marquee of Grauman's Chinese Theatre. Next to the imprints, she blocked out the words "Love to you all." At seven years and one month, she had become a Hollywood immortal.

The money rolled in. The studio paymaster made out her checks to her directly; then George Temple deposited them in her name in four of the best and safest places he knew: savings banks, U.S. government bonds, life insurance company annuities and bank-sponsored guaranteed trusts. George arranged to have her receive a share of the accumulated capital when she reached twenty-one and other shares at ten-year intervals until she was fifty. He also looked ahead and provided for her as-yet-unborn children.

The Temples were shrewd enough to say no to all the slick-tongue promoters and con artists who approached them with money-quadrupling schemes, and to the dozens of artists' representatives in Hollywood who promised them bigger and better contracts. They also turned down an offer by Arthur L. Bernstein, Jackie Coogan's stepfather, who, Gertrude said, walked up and down her living room one day "waving a check for half a million dollars in my face." Gertrude, unconvinced and cautious, needed advice. She turned, not to anybody who had made it big in Hollywood, but to a wise family physician. "He was the only professional man we knew," she explained. The doctor heard their story and said they were right: Say no.

By 1936, George was investing great sums for Shirley, though the little star herself received an allowance of just five dollars a week, which she stashed away in a little green metal strongbox her father gave her. That year her salary from her films was $121,422, which rose to $162,000 a year later. In 1938, she made $307,014, more money than the president of General Motors. Yet even this was not all; it does not include the royalties she was receiving from commercial companies that were marketing Shirley Temple *everythings*. By the time Shirley was twelve, her fortune was estimated at between three and five million dollars.

So great was her popularity that manufacturers correctly assumed she *could* sell anything that bore her name and likeness. Merchandisers bearing sample cases arrived by the dozens with products to show the Temples. As she had done with Shirley's film contracts, Gertrude made the deals, deciding which to endorse and for how much. She agreed to promotions for jewelry, china, soap, toys, dresses, coats, hats, shoes, storybooks, hair ribbons, purses, underwear and drinking mugs. At one time, contracts were granted to fifteen firms. In the seven years of Shirley's reign as the world's most popular child actress, fifteen million little girls wore Shirley Temple dresses.

Then there were the dolls, the biggest tie-in of them all and the most popular celebrity doll ever made.

A Talk With the Doll's Creator

Abe Katz admits to being "past ninety," but one must take his word for that. His face is pink and nearly smooth, his eyes are clear and his voice is strong.

Abe was in charge of producton at the Ideal Toy and Novelty Company in New York City, which manufactured the doll for the first time for the 1934 Christmas season. The doll was Ben Michtom's idea. Ben, the son of Morris Michtom, the company's founder and president, understood the importance of celebrity advertising. He had his brother-in-law, Murray Feil, who worked for the William Morris Agency in California, introduce him to Gertrude Temple.

Abe picks up the story: "There were months of negotiations before the deal was set. Mrs. Temple handled all the arrangements. Ben said she was very brilliant and sharp. Mr. Temple had nothing to do with it.

"We had doll bodies, but we needed the head. It had to look like Shirley Temple, but I didn't know what she looked like. So my wife and I went to a movie house in a section of Brooklyn called Bay Ridge where a Shirley Temple picture was playing so I could see her.

"Then we started to make the doll. The face was the most important thing. I wanted to get the right expression. I had a sculptor, Bernard Lipfert, work on the face. We had to make many different faces until I was satisfied. I'd think about it at night, get an inspiration, and the next day the factory would try to reproduce it.

"One of the problems was that the dolls were made of a wood pulp, sawdust and glue compressed into shape and put into a mold and baked under pressure. Well, the heat would sometimes make the materials run so the expression could change with the baking and we'd have to begin again. Nowadays they use plastic, so the expression is always the same.

"Also she had a dimple. We had to get that in just the right place, and that was some job. And the eyes. Most dolls were manufactured with blue or brown eyes. But Shirley's eyes were hazel and my doll had to have the same color. I had to make special arrangements with my supplier to give us hazel eyes.

"There were other problems. We needed a head with a lot of curls. But with the price of hair we couldn't afford to put on fifty-six curls and sell the doll for what we had planned. I decided to put about six or eight curls on each side and on top. The back was just combed down.

"After the factory had made some twenty molds, I felt I had a satsifactory likeness. I came home from work very happy. I told my wife to get a sitter for our three children and then we went to Morris Michtom's home over on Winthrop Street, with the Shirley doll in a brown paper bag. We drove past a group of young children and I stopped the car.

"I took the paper bag and went over to them. I pulled out the doll and showed it to them. 'What does this look like to you?' I asked.

" 'It's a doll.'

" 'Any special kind of doll?'

" 'Sure,' they said almost together, 'it's Shirley Temple.'

"So then I knew I had it.

"Well, we shipped that doll out to Los Angeles for Mrs. Temple's approval. She liked it and we put it into production right away. The first model was eighteen inches tall and sold for five dollars, a lot of money for those days. We dressed it up to look just like Shirley did in her "Baby Take a Bow" number, red-and-white organdy with polka dots, a full skirt, tight bodice and puffed sleeves, with a long red sash.

"Later on, when we made other dolls, we matched her outfits to Shirley's movies as they were made. We had her in a Civil War period costume, with pantalettes, when *The Littlest Rebel* came out, a two-piece blue-and-white sailor suit for *Captain January*, a tunic for *Wee Willie Winkie*.

"We thought we would make about ten thousand dolls that first season, but the orders kept coming and we had to make much more. We couldn't keep up, so we only took a certain amount of orders and promised them for after Christmas.

"Morris, our president, was happy as a lark. He even flew out to Los Angeles to deliver the first royalty check to Mrs. Temple personally. It was for seventy thousand dollars.

"At the house, Shirley sat on his knee. He liked that."

Morris liked the upwardly slanting sales charts even better as time went on. In a few years, Ideal sold more than six hundred thousand dolls and licensed companies to manufacture it all over the world. To meet the soaring demand, the company rented a large factory building in Long Island City and installed a block-long billboard on the roof with a huge picture of Shirley, illuminated at night by floodlights.

"The year before," Abe says, "the company had lost money. That doll gave us a big lift. Shirley took us right out of the Depression."

The family's life was changed utterly.

Gertrude continued to be at Shirley's side, receiving an increased salary every year. George was promoted to manager of his bank, which began to attract large numbers of children's savings accounts. In 1936, he was named to an executive post in a larger, more elegant branch of the California Bank at Hollywood and Cahuenga Boulevards, but he remained only a short while. He resigned to spend the rest of his life managing his daughter's business affairs.

Brother Jack, who turned twenty in 1936, was given a job as a publicity man in the studio but discovered after a few weeks that the only reason he was hired by Twentieth Century was his relationship to their high-earning star, so he quit and enrolled at Stanford University.

George Junior, then seventeen, went off to military school in New Mexico. One day a regular army officer inspecting his room spotted Shirley's picture on his wall. "Who," he asked, "is the Shirley Temple fan here?" George snapped off a salute and said "Me, sir." Asked to identify himself, he replied, "Cadet George Temple, sir." Meanwhile, from Palo Alto, Jack called and said he had been offered a role in a college play. Gertrude urged him to turn it down. "One of you in the family is enough," she argued.

Home was no longer the little bungalow on Twenty-fourth Street. It had given way to a larger house in Santa Monica, this one also stucco and tile-roofed, but with a two-car garage and an extra-large room that could be used as an office. There was a larger, less visible backyard where George had a playhouse constructed for Shirley, but, like the other, the home faced out upon a street. People walked by and even peered into the front windows; cars stopped at all hours, discharging passengers who would snap pictures and move on; the Temples were stopped each time they left and entered.

Shirley's room was large and bright, decorated with pictures of her as Little Bo-Peep with the lambs wagging their tails behind them. In the early evening, George Temple would sit there with her, take her on his lap and tell her, "Someday, we'll have a beautiful big home and a beautiful big playroom, just for you."

The day came quickly.

In 1936, the Temples began searching for a place upon which to erect the big, beautiful house. On weekends they drove around the Los Angeles area, and one day, in Brentwood, they saw a large plot of ground. As they walked around inspecting it, they passed a bush out of which came a mother and father quail, followed single-file by a number of baby quail. Shirley was entranced. "This is the place," she announced.

The Temples liked the secluded, wooden site on a hillside, and that year they took their big leap upscale. They used part of Shirley's earnings to purchase the lot, where they had architect John Byers design a new house.

It was large but quite unlike the showy mansions of some of Hollywood's reigning stars. A blend of English and Normandy farmhouse styles, it was lovely and unpretentious. Unseen from the road, it sat on a rise overlooking the Will Rogers Memorial Polo Grounds. For extra protection, a high wall encircled the property, with a gate that opened and closed at the touch of a button. When they drove home in the evening, the Temples could lean out of their car window and put a key into the lock, and the gates would spring apart for them.

Within the parklike setting at 209 South Rockingham Avenue was everything any little girl could wish for from a bottled genie.

There was a swimming pool, most of its long length only a foot or two deep, and next to it a badminton court. An electrically driven merry-go-round was nearby, and a short distance from the

65

house there was a stable which housed two ponies, one called Spunky, another Little Carnation, plus a horse for Shirley's brother George. Also in the stable were Shirley's two dogs, Rowdy, a cocker spaniel, and Corky, a Scottie. A third, a Pekingese named Ching-Ching, lived in the house.

Shirley slept in a red-and-white bedroom-and-nursery suite on the second floor. Through a floor-to-ceiling bay window with a skylight roof, she could see the broad blue Pacific a few miles away. The furnishings were practical, sturdy, long-wearing—and Shirley-size, from the twin beds (she slept in one and piled the other with toys) to the sofa, chairs and closets. The closets were filled with dresses for all occasions. There was also a private dressing room equipped with a full-length mirror and a vanity with a light-bordered mirror. In her suite, too, was a large glassed cabinet in which she placed the dolls she received from admirers throughout the world. (Eventually they would be moved to the playhouse, where they would continue to multiply until there were about fifteen hundred in all.)

Then there was the playhouse.

Down the hill from the main building, with its own driveway and shielded by high shrubbery, was an English-style cottage the size of a home in a middle-income suburb, but far more luxuriously appointed.

Its outstanding feature was a vast room fifty feet long and forty feet wide, with a two-story vaulted ceiling. Along one wall was a huge recessed fireplace; at one end was a stage with a hidden motion picture screen, at the other a soda fountain. The latter was equipped with stools, chrome-and-marble spigots which squirted syrups and carbonated water, jars of toppings, and chests containing ice cream. The playhouse also contained a vast wardrobe in which were kept all the costumes and uniforms she wore in her movies. Later, a full-size bowling alley was added in the basement.

This was Shirley's indoor play area where she had parties for her selected guests, showed movies or went to be alone.

Gertrude and George Temple never matched their personal lifestyle to their luxurious surroundings. They stayed home most evenings, avoiding the Hollywood scene almost entirely. They hired a cook-housekeeper-maid, a part-time gardener to take care of the grounds, and one full-time and one part-time secretary to answer the fan mail.

There was also a personal bodyguard/chauffeur, assigned to Shirley by Zanuck himself and paid by the studio. He was brawny Johnny Griffith, who, as a boy, had saved young Darryl's life when both cut school one day to go swimming in the Elkhorn River, which cuts through northeast Nebraska where both were raised. Years later, when Johnny found himself out of work in California, he went to see Zanuck, who put him to work as Shirley's special protector.

Grif remained with Shirley until she grew up, hovering around the Brentwood house, driving her to the studio, accompanying her on trips and permitting his charge to play with his handcuffs. In a book she wrote in 1945, Shirley tells how Grif could be persuaded to part with those cuffs. "You could beg them away from Grif," she says, "and handcuff people to chairs or handcuff yourself." Once she got William A. Seiter, who directed her in the films *Dimples*, *Stowaway* and *Susannah of the Mounties*, to lie prone and allow himself to be handcuffed. Seiter, a realistic actor, pretended to struggle and moan, to Shirley's delight, but enough was enough after a while and he asked to be set loose. Shirley, however, was not yet ready to end the game. She had given the key to a property man who was a buddy, with instructions to keep it hidden. Seiter remained in shackles until he bellowed to be freed. "Unfortunately," Shirley said, "his authority over the propman was such that the key had to be given back."

Schooling, no problem for Shirley, was sometimes a headache for her studio. Under California law, professional children could work only six hours a day and had to receive a total of three hours' instruction from a teacher licensed by the Board of Education. Thus, when the time came for Shirley to attend school, Frances Klampt arrived on the scene, remaining until 1939.

Miss Klampt, a dark-haired young woman with a pleasant round face, looked retiring, even timid, but was not. A teacher for five years before her appointment as tutor, she took seriously her mandate to be in full charge of the education of Shirley Temple.

The law made clear that she represented both the Los Angeles Board of Education and the Child Labor Board and thus had unquestioned authority to halt whatever was going on if, in her sole judgment, something was occurring on the set which she felt might be harmful to her pupil. Miss Klampt clocked Shirley in every morning and kept a chart of hours studied. Sometimes, when the shooting schedule was unusually tight, she would permit the directors to borrow an hour, but it had to be made up in a day or two.

A regulation school desk and chair were moved into Shirley's bungalow, where Miss Klampt—"Klammie" to the star—taught her the regular public-school curriculum from state-issued textbooks and gave her the approved examinations.

Although Shirley was a good student, there were times when Miss Klampt found she had fallen behind. She would thereupon march up to the director, inform him that more time was needed, and return to the bungalow, where, seated at a small desk, Shirley would try to find Minnesota on a map or figure out how much was 105 times six. Once, when Miss Klampt was drilling her in arithmetic, the company manager was making his own computations. Mournfully, he told author McEvoy that the two-hour delay in production had cost the studio five thousand dollars.

Klammie was especially alert to bad language spoken where Shirley could hear. So in fact, were her directors. Once John Ford, directing *Wee Willie Winkie*, overheard a member of the crew utter a swear word. He pointed to the man—"You!"—then to a corner, where he made the offender stand for several minutes, his back to the set.

On one occasion, Shirley herself was responsible for causing Lionel Barrymore to erupt. The eldest of the great acting family had balked at playing with Shirley to begin with. David Butler, assigned to direct a movie about the Old South called *The Little Colonel*, had gone to the actor's dressing room at the Metro-Goldwyn-Mayer studio. Butler, who had worked with Barrymore and knew him well, got a firm refusal at first. "I've heard about her," said Lionel, "and I don't want to do it."

"Lionel," Butler insisted, "you've done everything in the theater, everything in pictures, and you're one of the best actors in the world. Yow owe it to yourself to work with this little girl, because she's marvelous and you'll love her." Barrymore grumpily agreed, and promptly regretted it.

In the story, set in the post–Civil War South, Shirley comes to live with her crotchety grandfather, who is estranged from her mother because she married a hated Northerner. In the scene that got Lionel's goat, he and Shirley play a board game in his den, using Northern and Southern soldiers as counters. As the cameras ground, Barrymore said, "If I were doing that, I'd move right here and put my man here." Shirley, following the script, replied, "If you did that, I'd jump you here and jump you there."

Barrymore frowned; he'd forgotten what came next. Stopping the action, he called out, "What are my lines?"

Shirley spoke up. "Oh, Uncle Lionel," she said, "you have to say . . ." And she proceeded to tell him, perfectly, what was in the script. Barrymore, unaccustomed to being prompted by a seven-year-old, and his tolerance at low ebb anyway because of severe arthritis, unleashed a blistering stream of profanity.

Klammie bolted forward like a shot. Reproving Barrymore for his "bad language," she grasped Shirley by the hand and marched her off the set. Barrymore stared, Butler's mouth fell open. There was no appeal. Klammie took Shirley home, and the film had to be shot without the star the rest of the day.

Visitors arrived from all over the world to see Shirley make her movies and talk to her on the set. There were so many the directors ordered the gates shut and only the very important were admitted. Shirley was not overly impressed by even the most glittering names. Says one director, "Those who did manage to get in usually said the same things. They'd spot her and exclaim, 'Oh, there she is. Oh, what a darling!' Then they'd say, these big, big shots, 'Come here.' Shirley would look at them as if to say, Who the hell are you? She would look at her mother, and her mother would give a nod, and then she would go up to the lady or gentleman and curtsy. With men, she'd shake hands."

J. Edgar Hoover, in the early years of his long tenure as director of the Federal Bureau of Investigation, was an ardent fan. The studio admitted him. He was one of the few she knew about, and they had a fine chat. After a visit by H. G. Wells, she was told that the eminent British novelist was one of the most important persons anyone could know. She replied: "No, God is the most important. And the governor of California is second." When the remark was repeated to Zanuck he reportedly observed, "Didn't you ask her who was third?"

Once she got George Murphy to do imitations for Mrs. Roosevelt on the set of *Little Miss Broadway*. That morning, Shirley had been cautioned by the publicity department not to delay the President's wife overlong, because she was on a very tight schedule. When she came, however, Shirley took her by the hand and led her to her bungalow, where they remained for a half hour.

Soon she popped her head out the door and called to George. "Murph," she said as he approached, "do *East Lynne* for Mrs. Roosevelt. I told her you were great." Murphy looked startled. "While waiting for our scenes," he recalled later, "I'd do comic imitations to amuse Shirley, and this *East Lynne* routine was one of them. Well, it was okay for Shirley, but the President's wife!" Shirley insisted, and, as Mrs. Roosevelt looked on grinning, Murphy went through the bit, feeling foolish but earning their applause when it was finished.

On rare occasions, Shirley went calling. Once she was taken to visit General John J. Pershing in his Palm Springs home. "Black Jack," then nearing eighty, was plainly captivated, but unfortunately the enchantment was not mutual. During their meeting, Shirley showed him her prized autograph book signed by stars. When she asked if he was personally acquainted with any of them, Pershing had to confess he was not and that, moreover, he had not heard of most. Shirley looked at him in perplexity. After she left, she asked a studio aide, "How did he ever get to be a general?"

7
Newsmaker

She was the most public child ever reared in America.

Moviegoers knew everything about her: what she ate and how much, how she spent her time, what she wore, read, liked, hated. That she never had mumps, measles, chicken pox and other diseases of childhood. Kids repeated Shirley jokes. ("How's the tailoring business?" "So-so.") Psychologists wrote articles in national magazines evaluating her chances of growing up unspoiled.

Every mother knew that Shirley sucked her thumb until she was two and that Mrs. Temple despaired of stopping her until she hit upon the idea of tying the thumb from an old glove on her hand and instructed her to "keep it clean." Thousands then tried the same trick. Gertrude also halted the nail-biting habit for uncounted numbers of children by disclosing that she painted Shirley's nails with natural polish.

The press snapped her picture unceasingly. In the year when such figures as FDR, Mohandas Gandhi, Charles Lindbergh and Edward VIII and Wallis Simpson strode the world stage, she was said to be the world's most photographed person. Early in her career, during an interview, she glanced at a large pile of magazines on a coffee table. "I'll bet you a nickel," she told the writer, "that if you pick up any one of those magazines, my picture will be in it." The writer got the wager down to a penny, chose a periodical from the middle of the stack and turned the pages. Sure enough, her photograph was there.

Although Shirley needed no press agentry to get public attention, she got it anyway. Her studio lost no opportunity to merchandise her, beginning where it did with other female stars, lopping a year off her age. Everyone was taken in, including Shirley, who learned on her twelfth birthday that she was actually thirteen. In 1936, *Time* magazine in a cover article wrote: "Unlike most cinema actresses, Shirley Temple does not conceal the date of her birth. It was April 23, 1929." She didn't, they did: the year was 1928. The studio undoubtedly felt that what was precocious in a five-year-old would be even more so if the child were only four. A birth announcement card, similar to those sold in stationery stores, gave the 1929 birth date. The real birth certificate was later ferreted out by the press.

A surefire way of getting newspaper attention, second only to a romance, was The Feud, which is still employed by less-imaginative flacks when all else fails to win space. Publicists decided to create a battle with Jane Withers, the round-faced tomboy with the straight dark hair who appeared with Shirley in *Bright Eyes*. Pictures were released showing Shirley on a bike and Jane, in the background, sticking out her tongue.

Studio personnel who asked not to be identified said Jane had been hand-picked for the film by Gertrude Temple, who felt she was plain enough not to be a threat to Shirley. However, David Butler, who directed *Bright Eyes*, takes credit for the casting of Jane, who, he says, virtually talked her way into the part of the bratty rich kid who would be an abrasive foil for Shirley.

"We had about thirty kids that I had to interview," he says. "The mothers would bring the kids in and sit in the waiting room. The first one they brought in was Jane Withers.

"She came in, full of pep. She said, 'How are you, Mr. Butler.'

"'Fine, what have you done in pictures?'

"She said, 'I can give a lot of imitations.' And she started to give an imitation of Greta Garbo and this one and that one. She said, 'I can do anything,' and was talking all the time. She was perfect. So I said to my assistant, 'Take this girl and her mother up to the office and sign her, and let the other people go.' Boy, there was a riot around there. They wanted to kill me, because I sent them all home."

Withers, who was outstandingly obnoxious as Joyce Smythe, became the second—after Shirley—hottest child star. In the film, she delivers two classic lines, one when she expresses disgust because she did not receive what she wanted most for Christmas, a machine gun, and the other when she tells Shirley, "There ain't no Santa Claus, because my psychiatrist says so."

Emphatically, she denies any feud. It was, she says, a creation of the publicity department. "As far as I was concerned, it was a lot of bunk," Withers said. "There never was one."

The most ludicrous example of press agentry concerned Shirley and Santa Claus.

Children, the flacks at Twentieth-Century reasoned, believed in Santa. Shirley was a child. Hence it had to follow that Shirley must believe in Santa Claus—at least so far as the public was concerned. Whether she did or not in private apparently made little difference.

Shirley says she stopped believing in Santa Claus when she was a youngster because the department store Santa her mother took her to see asked for an autograph. The two had lined up with a crowd of youngsters, who were as excited to see Shirley as they were about Santa. When Shirley's turn came, Santa pulled her on his lap and whispered to her. Indignantly, Shirley wriggled off and whispered to her mother that he couldn't be the real Santa. "He asked for my autograph and said he saw all my movies," she complained.

Despite her loss of innocence, her Christmas requests were made public each year. At six, she asked Santa for a midget automobile and offered to "trade you an autographed picture of myself and Ronald Colman for one of yours."

In January of 1939, when she was almost eleven years old, a time when young girls' attention turns to more worldly concerns, *Photoplay* magazine published Shirley's "letter to Santa," illustrating the article with a picture of a handwritten message. Squeezing the last ounce of publicity from a waning childhood, Shirley's "letter," which the publication had to admit was her "last" to Santa, asked for a baby doll to replace one which had been broken and buried in her backyard "because the doll hospital couldn't fix it," a pair of blue dungarees, a blue-and-red checked cowboy shirt and a pair of six-shooters. She also apologized for putting a bell on the toe of her stocking the previous year in an attempt to sound an alarm which would awaken her when he appeared. There were no more "letters to Santa" after that.

Inevitably Shirley's phenomenal success spawned some ridiculous rumors. Shirley was really a thirty-year-old midget with two children, a British magazine declared, a "scoop" also headlined in the Italian press. George carried Shirley's birth certificate in his wallet, showing it to all who asked about the rumor, which died a natural death as Shirley grew older and taller. Another story "revealed" that an electrified fence surrounded the Temples' Brentwood home to shock intruders. Gertrude explained, sensibly, that such a fence would be just as likely to electrocute Shirley and her guests.

In 1937, Shirley made news of a different sort in a celebrated libel action. A suit was filed on her behalf against a British publication and novelist Graham Greene, then thirty-four years old. In his review of *Wee Willie Winkie*, Greene, film critic for a British magazine called *Night and Day* which sought to be a kind of British *New Yorker*, discussed Shirley's appeal in sexual terms. According to the statement of claim filed in King's Bench Division, he accused 20th Century–Fox of "procuring" Shirley Temple "for immoral purposes." When his review was published, *Night and Day* announced the article with a poster: "Sex and Shirley Temple," which was displayed in court.

The Temples and 20th Century–Fox of the U.S. and Britain sued Greene, the magazine, its printers and its publishers, and won a settlement. When the case was heard, Sir Patrick Hastings, counsel for the plaintiffs, announced that the settlement called for the payment of £2,000 (about $10,000 at the time) to Shirley and £1,000 and £500 pounds respectively to the American and British film companies. Sir Patrick refused to read what he called "the beastly publication" in court but said it was "one of the most horrible libels one can imagine about a child nine years of age." Lord Chief Justice Hewart, hearing the case, stated, "This libel is simply a gross outrage."

At the time, Shirley probably knew nothing of the storm swirling around her. She did not, of course, appear in court; neither did Greene, who was in Mexico on a writing assignment. *Night and Day* lasted only six months. Greene said he kept the statement of claim on his bathroom wall until a German bomb "removed" both statement and wall during the blitz.

Shirley's remarkable ability to generate news without benefit of studio mimeograph machines was demonstrated anew in the summer of 1938 when, with no filming scheduled until fall, the Temples decided to take her on her first cross-country automobile trip. Her studio agreed but insisted that she be accompanied by her bodyguard Grif and, as insurance in case the press needed some prodding along the route, a publicity man.

She drew crowds everywhere. In Harp, Kansas, the manager of the hotel where they stopped for the night wanted to see Shirley so much that he kept returning to her room with armfuls of towels and bars of guest soap. Gertrude finally told him they had enough. A national magazine posed her in a field of wheat for its cover. Later, the Temples received a letter from a farmer saying he recognized the wheat as his and asking to be paid for its use.

After a triumphant month en route, they reached the nation's capital. The Temples were resting in their suite in the Mayflower Hotel when the telephone rang. President Roosevelt was calling. He wanted to see Shirley. "Could you bring her over?" an aide asked. Gertrude stammered that they could. She hung up and rang room service and ordered up a quick lunch. It arrived in minutes.

Shirley bit into a sandwich. Disaster! Out came a front tooth which had been threatening to do just that for several days.

"My glamor evaporated," Shirley said later. "We had to leave immediately, so nothing could be done to fix me up." She remembered being awed by the magnificence of the White House, a feeling which left when Roosevelt shook her hand and grinned.

"Unfortunately I couldn't smile back," Shirley said. Roosevelt sensed that something was wrong and asked if she was nervous, so Shirley revealed the story of the lost tooth. "He rocked back in his chair and chuckled the way I always imagined Santa Claus would chuckle. Then he confided he was missing quite a few himself."

It was an exceptionally busy day at the White House. Secretary of the Treasury Henry Morgenthau was waiting in the anteroom. Roosevelt himself was in the midst of preparations for a nation-wide broadcast that evening which had been heralded as the opening gun of his 1940 campaign for a third term. He would call upon the nation's voters, specifically members of the Republican Party, to cut old ties and back his New Deal program. Think "liberal and conservative" instead, he exhorted.

He took time out, however, to chat with Shirley about lamb chops. She had eaten some that week and she described them in detail to Roosevelt, who listened attentively.

Shirley told waiting reporters Roosevelt had spoken about Sistie and Buzzie (Anna Eleanor and Curtis Roosevelt Dahl), his grandchildren, and she had related how she caught an eleven-pound salmon off Vancouver Island. When reporters revealed that Mr. Morgenthau had been waiting, Shirley protested, "But what *we* were talking about was important." She pronounced FDR "one of the nicest people I know" and showed them her autograph book. He had signed his name on the same page as Eleanor Roosevelt had when she visited her movie set.

"To Shirley," the President had written, "from her old friend, Franklin D. Roosevelt."

She was ten, with the poise, self-control and manner of a fifteen-year-old. In New York she held court for the sons and daughters of newspapermen who were invited to her hotel suite. Columnist Walter Winchell's daughter was invited to spend the night. Shirley also did some sightseeing: a chartered boat took her around Manhattan Island and to the Statue of Liberty, and she was driven through the Wall Street area and around Harlem.

Movie-star Shirley had never been to a legitimate theater, so she was taken to the matinee performances of *What a Life* and *I Married An Angel*. Backstage with star Vera Zorina, she inquired, "Could I see your wings?" They were brought out for examination. A veteran of the movie set with its multiplicity of cameras and sound equipment, she wanted to know where the microphones were hidden.

One afternoon she went shopping in the Waldorf-Astoria jewelry shop of Roy W. Johnson, which merited a press release informing Shirley-watchers that she chose six gold charms for her bracelet—a tiny Victrola with doors that opened to reveal a record, a gold mesh purse, a working compass, an hourglass filled with colored sand, a church with a steeple, and a Punch and Judy show. She really wanted to buy a gift for her mother, it was said but, after examining some diamond clips and brooches, concluded that the ten dollars she had saved would not be enough.

Eleanor Roosevelt invited Shirley and her parents to a picnic at Valkill, her private cottage on the Hyde Park estate of the President. On a hot July day, George Temple drove to Poughkeepsie, Shirley beside him in a short-sleeved white shirt and tan suspender-strapped shorts, her blond curls bound up in a yellow print scarf. Gertrude was in the back seat. Word of Shirley's impending arrival had reached the area's younger people. Several hundred boys and girls were gathered at New Market Street, where they gazed curiously while the Temples picked up a state trooper who led them in an open car along the bumpy two-and-a-half-mile road to the cottage.

Eleven-year-old Sistie, and Buzzie, eight, were waiting with their grandmother outside the cottage. Scores of newspaper and newsreel cameras were on hand, but Twentieth Century–Fox had decreed that only the studio's photographer be permitted inside the grounds.

Shirley, a thorough professional even on vacation, instructed the First Lady on posing techniques. "I was amused," wrote Mrs. Roosevelt in her syndicated column, "My Day," "when we walked out together for the first picture to have her tell me just what to do. 'We should walk from far back and wave at the cameras as we come out.' When I did not realize the camera was following us, she said, 'They are still taking us' and we turned for a final wave together."

Lunch was outdoors—lamb chops, broiled by Mrs. Roosevelt herself on a charcoal grill, salad, potato chips and ice cream and fresh raspberries, sent over by Secretary and Mrs. Morgenthau.

Years later Shirley told how the sight of Mrs. Roosevelt bending over the chops triggered an uncontrollable impulse. She slipped her favorite toy, a slingshot which accompanied her everywhere, out of her pocket and aimed a pebble at Mrs. Roosevelt's rear. "I couldn't resist," she said.

She didn't and let fly. Mrs. Roosevelt jumped. The Secret Service men, somewhat abashed, were unable to find the perpetrator, but Gertrude knew her daughter.

"She didn't blow the whistle on me until we got back to the hotel," Shirley recalled. "Then she let me have it in the same area where I had attacked the First Lady."

After lunch, Mrs. Roosevelt donned a navy-blue bathing suit and announced it was hot enough for a swim in the pool. Shirley declined to join the others "because of my hair." She inquired about the whereabouts of the two police badges she had given Mrs. Roosevelt on the studio set and was only slightly mollified to learn they were now the proud possessions of Sistie and Buzzie.

After visiting the "big house," where they were introduced to Mrs. Sara Delano Roosevelt, the President's mother, the Temples got into their sedan for the drive back to New York. She told reporters waiting at the end of the driveway she had had a "swell time."

The next day, Mrs. Roosevelt devoted her entire column to Shirley's visit. In glowing terms, she wrote that Shirley was "a well brought-up, charming child" who was "a joy to all who meet her." She harbored no suspicion that it was Shirley who had pinged her in the behind.

New York State's governor, Herbert H. Lehman, and his wife entertained the Temples at a lawn party at their Purchase, New York, summer home. The Lehman children, John and Hilda Jane, and Shirley played leapfrog and she distributed some more police badges. Later she disregarded her coiffure and went swimming with the governor—even though it took forty minutes for the curls to dry.

The press found no detail of her journey too inconsequential, no conversation too trivial. They printed every bit of information they could get—and the public ate it up.

Little wonder that *The New York Times*, while declaring that "we stand second to none in our admiration for Shirley," nevertheless put its editorial tongue in cheek and found it a "painful duty to report that there are a few curmudgeonly old home-bodies and stick-in-the-muds who are getting just a little allergic to Shirley." Wrote the *Times*:

> These benighted souls feel that if she is allowed to swarm all over this Atlantic seaboard, cheered on by her unchallenged press department, she will sooner or later take over the entire United States, including the "templed hills" prophetically mentioned in the grand old anthem *America*.
>
> This is a despicable attitude. What could be more touching than to read of Shirley's discussion with President Roosevelt of lamb chops and her lost tooth? Any one can see they are intimately related topics. What could be more winning than her pretty hesitation at the Hyde Park swimming pool for fear of getting her hair wet and not being able to do a thing with it? And how delightful to note how she "stole" the Westchester Horse Show! How amusing to observe how she took over the hat-check concession at a children's (liquorless) cocktail party and refused to accept a single tip!
>
> The disaffected old-fogy minority, of course, has a reply. They insist that the only thing more touching, winning, delightful and amusing than reading about all this is not reading about it. They say Shirley belongs on the screen in charge of a good director. Shame on them! Shirley belongs in the very spot into which she has hurled herself—right in the great big, soft-shelled heart of America.

All this, however, was eclipsed by the Boston experience when Shirley developed a stomachache and upset the whole world.

The Temples were staying at the elegant Ritz-Carlton Hotel when Shirley complained she didn't feel well. Quickly she was put to bed and the doctor summoned. Newspersons came racing to the hotel, jamming the lobby and spilling out into Arlington Street. After conferring with Mrs. Temple, Ed Wyner, owner of the hotel, turned the sample room into a press office where Gertrude and the two physicians treating Shirley presided over daily briefings. Gertrude endeared herself to the reporters by ordering coffee and sandwiches to be sent to them hourly.

For five days bulletins about Shirley's condition were flashed to all continents. Unwilling to wait for the wire service reports, the *London Daily Mirror* called each day, at high transatlantic rates. When Shirley's temperature hit 103.5, the *Christian Science Monitor* ran her picture on the front page. Boston papers assigned reporters to the story in eight-hour shifts around the clock. One enterprising photographer set up his camera in the Public Garden across from the hotel and started a group of children chanting, "We want Shirley!" under her window. Shirley, hearing them, popped out of bed and looked out. The cameraman snapped her picture.

Back in Hollywood, the public-relations people weren't about to let any opportunities slip by. While the East Coast waited for the daily briefings, the West found an omen from the heavens. Raymond Dannenbaum of the 20th Century–Fox publicity department told reporters about it. When Shirley's fever finally broke, he said, a white dove fluttered down from the blue sky to land on the shoulder of the Temples' Brentwood estate caretaker. He brought it straight to the public-relations department, which immediately called a news conference to share the good news with the world.

The Temples had barely unpacked back home in Los Angeles when Shirley once again made international headlines, this time in a bizarre episode. Martin Dies, a six-foot-three, rangy Texas congressman who was chairman of the House Committee on Un-American Activities, was conducting an investigation to search out Communists in American life. At a hearing in Washington on August 22, he obtained testimony from J. B. Matthews, a self-appointed authority on the penetration of Communists in the country's midst, that Shirley had done a great service to "the cause." Matthews told a packed hearing room that Shirley, along with Clark Gable, James Cagney, Bette Davis and some others, had sent a message of greetings to a French Communist newspaper. While Matthews stopped short of calling Shirley and the others Communists, saying only that the "hearty greetings" ascribed to her had been sent "unwittingly," he had nevertheless given the impression that she and the others had unknowingly been dupes.

The irony was that Shirley Temple's family, and Shirley herself in later years, always were staunch Republicans and political conservatives. The utter absurdity of the testimony was underscored by Harold L. Ickes, FDR's ascerbic Secretary of the Interior, who observed with heavy sarcasm in a speech to the Tacoma Young Men's Republican Club, "I find that while I was in Alaska the Red hunters swung into action again. They even went to Hollywood and made the amazing discovery that little Shirley Temple is a dangerous Red. Imagine the great committee raiding her nursery and seizing her dolls as evidence. It is all so very silly." Old Iron Pants received a thunderous ovation. Secretary of Labor Frances Perkins added her own barrage, asserting that Shirley was lucky to have been born in this country; otherwise, she said, Martin Dies would have sought her deportation.

Dies earned nationwide ridicule. A jingle was sung around the country to the tune of "My Darling Clementine":

> Down in Texas, in the Badlands,
> Where the mighty Rio flows,
> Martin Di-es went to Congress—
> And the Nation held its nose.
>
> Shirley Temple is a Commie,
> This I really know is true.
> She will tear you all to pieces
> With her dangerous boo-hoo-hoo!

8
Profile at Ten

By the end of 1938, with Shirley ten years old and at the apex of her career, she had starred in seventeen pictures, each a solid success. Allan Dwan, who directed her that year in *Rebecca of Sunnybrook Farm*, describes her appearance: "She was just a trifle short for her age, with a sturdy little body on equally sturdy though well-shaped legs, lovely hazel eyes, a round little face with that great dimple still there and skin that simply glowed. The hair was gold-colored, a darkish gold, and the curls were finally gone. About time, because she had outgrown her baby days. We had them part her hair on the left side and tie it back on the right. It made her look older and yet still a child. She was pretty, but you could not call her beautiful, not the beauty that Elizabeth Taylor was as a child or, to come up to the present, Brooke Shields."

She was extraordinarily gifted, yet with a child's interests, enthusiasms and emotions. Zanuck summed up the two sides of her personality this way: He admitted he was uncomfortable in her presence because "I feel that her intellect is so superior to mine." He added, "If I told her to ice-skate for a picture, she'd probably be doing all of Sonja Henie's tricks within a couple of days." At the same time, he found the child in her emerging constantly. "My children get along with her famously," he sighed, "except when they're squabbling over toys."

She was leading a childhood that, for all of her parents' efforts, was not a normal one. It could not be, a fact Gertrude clearly recognized. J. P. McAvoy writes: "She realized that her little girl had to be protected from her own popularity, that she could never lead a normal little-girl life in public, for the public wouldn't let her."

Each day, when she left the studio, she had to be driven home in a bulletproof limousine to a house bristling with protective devices and encircled by a high wall. The entrance roadway was wired with hidden alarms, connected to the police station, that gave instant warning of intruders. Inside the house, she looked out through barred windows, which were also linked to an alarm system. J. Edgar Hoover himself had come out to supervise installation of the elaborate protective devices. Around the grounds, patrolling constantly, were guards carrying revolvers.

Noting all this, Harriet Parsons, a movie producer and daughter of the Hearst columnist Louella O. Parsons, says, "How could this child have had a normal childhood? It simply wasn't possible." Dorothy Manners, who took over the Parsons column after serving for years as Louella's assistant, is blunt: "It was awful for Shirley." Jackie Cooper, speaking from the experience of a former child sensation, told these writers, "No kid in our position can have a childhood at all, much less a normal one."

Dwan says, "She didn't have freedom of life. She lived pretty tight at home, tighter than at the studio." Whenever he visited the home to discuss a current movie with Gertrude, Shirley would hover near, listening. "She seemed like a kid in a convent or a private school, as if she were taking lessons from the qualified teachers who lived there," said Dwan. To him, the home was an after-hours version of the movie set. "Whatever they talked about had to do with the studio."

As adults find it difficult to forget their work after hours, Shirley did, too. The vocabulary of the studio, its importance, its personalities became a part of her, as the following story makes clear.

One day at a tea party at her home, she was the only child in a roomful of grown-up guests. During the afternoon, they played a word game which required participants to pack a trunk with an alphabetical list of objects. Thus the first player would say, "I put an apple into my trunk." The second must repeat "apple," then supply an object beginning with the letter *b*.

The letter *g* fell to Shirley. Quickly she offered her word, "gags," a movie term. A guest got *m*, hesitated and was prompted by Shirley. "Money," she whispered. When the game ended before the end of the alphabet was reached, she was disappointed. "I had such a good one for *z*, she said. Asked what it was, she replied, "Zanuck."

Still, she was sunny of disposition, cheerful and bursting with energy. She was self-sufficient, able to be her own good companion. She could play for long periods by herself without boredom, drawing with her crayons and paints, attending to the animals she loved, sitting and reading.

At the studio, her closets were filled with dresses, each one beautiful; she would put them on, take them off, as she pleased. At home, her doll collection was growing rapidly, but faster still grew her arsenal: she had an enormous number of toy guns, possibly the best in the U.S., among them a make-believe submachine gun sent to her by J. Edgar Hoover. It was a toss-up which collection she enjoyed most.

The fact that she *could* play by herself was salutary, even essential, because the isolation from much of the real world that was imposed upon her by the studio could easily have damaged her personality, as it has harmed and even wrecked the lives of so many other child stars.

The youthful actors who performed with Shirley in her films quickly became aware of her insulation. A number of those interviewed saw her as alone on a mountaintop, lonely and inaccessible. Young and high-spirited themselves, unconstrained because they were not multimillion-dollar "properties," they could not understand why there was such a high fence around Shirley.

Delmar Watson, who was Shirley's own choice to play the role of Peter the goatherd in *Heidi*, is now fifty-five years old, a commercial photographer in Los Angeles.

Watson: "I worked with Shirley in *To the Last Man*, her first really full-length movie back in 1933. We were great friends. I carried her suitcase from the bus to the hotel when we went on location. We were just like brother and sister, had lots of fun playing together. We would draw pictures and chase each other around. I was all of seven and she was about five.

"Then, in *Heidi*, things changed a lot. There was a call for auditions for the part of Peter, and about twenty kids were chosen and lined up and Allan Dwan went from one to another, talking to each one, asking questions, noting voice quality and stage presence. As he was doing this, Shirley came on the set. Mr. Dwan called her over.

"'Which one of these boys would you like to play Peter with you?' he asked her. Shirley very shyly stuck out a hand and pointed toward me, and I got the part.

"Now things were different from those early days, a lot different. We went on location at Lake Arrowhead. It was in the summer, the days were pleasant and I had a grand time playing in the hills between takes, joking with the grips and other technicians, tossing horseshoes with them. Shirley's trailer home was parked on the side of a hill. She was there all the time with her bodyguard and, of course, her mother. Only a few studio people were allowed up there.

"Shirley had a stand-in for the sound and lights. Then, when everything was set, she'd be called. She would come down at the last minute, we'd do our scene together and when it was finished she would be escorted back up the hill and disappear into the trailer. We'd never see her at any other time. We'd all have lunch in some big building they made into a commissary, but Shirley would always eat by herself in her trailer.

"Once I was playing horseshoes right after lunch with the lighting guys and she came out of her trailer. I said, 'Hi' and she greeted me and asked if she could play. Sure, we told her. She picked up a horseshoe and tossed it. I think she missed. She played with us for exactly two minutes, and then her bodyguard came down and took her away, back up the hill into the trailer. I heard him tell her she wasn't supposed to be there. As she left, I said to her, 'Bye. Maybe you can do it later.' Shirley didn't say anything but obediently returned to the trailer.

"I felt so darned sorry for her. She seemed so lonely. The studio executives didn't want her to get sunburned or take any chances that she might get hurt or be bothered by people, so they kept her away from everybody. There she was, a big star, and no chance of having any fun. I always felt she was almost like the character she had played in her movie two years before, *Poor Little Rich Girl,* in which she was the daughter of a soap tycoon who didn't have any time for her."

The isolation had already begun four years earlier during the filming of *Bright Eyes,* the first star vehicle concocted especially for Shirley, and the movie in which she sang the number that would follow her forever, "On the Good Ship *Lollipop.*"

On the set, Jane Withers, who had a leading role, was kept away from Shirley in free time.

Withers: "We never spoke to each other. We worked together in a scene but never played or talked together until after I was fifteen years old. Her childhood sure was different from mine, and I had a marvelous one. I used to feel very upset as a small child working with her. I was very concerned about her. I liked her and cared about her, and I didn't think she was having a very good time. I couldn't understand, there was such a wild difference between us. She was extremely professional, did everything she was told. It used to bother me. I said to my mother, 'Mama, she doesn't act like a kid, like a child, and I don't think she is having very much of a good time like I am.' I longed to talk to her about it.

"I liked her so much and I thought she was the most talented [actress]. She was so adorable and so beautiful. I wanted to go up and give her a bear hug and say, 'Look, kid, I'd give anything in the world to talk to you, but I was told I can't.' My mother thought it was ridiculous. She was appalled when the assistant director said I couldn't talk or play with her except when we were in a scene."

It wasn't until each had entered the teens that they spoke, and then, Jane says, they would double-date. "I was so thrilled," she asserts. "So many prayers were answered for me when I finally had some time to share some thoughts with her." They have not seen each other in years, but Jane still considers Shirley the "number-one child star in the world."

Each year studio bosses threw a big party on Shirley's birthday on the lot, inviting 150 to 200 children, who came all dressed up, dived into the mountains of cake and ice cream, played games and watched the entertainers. Shirley was there and, of course, so were the reporters and cameramen. When she turned fifty, Shirley remembered these gala affairs and admitted that most of her guests were total strangers to her. "They were children of people at the studio," she said, "newspaper reporters and editors. It was fun but impersonal."

When it was all over, she would go home and have her real birthday party, just with her family.

However, it would be a mistake to assume that Shirley was bothered about the isolation imposed by the studio. Movie-making was a "game" she adored. "I have enjoyed every instant of my life as Shirley Temple," she wrote in *The American Weekly*, "and in spite of all the adjustments I had to make, and still do, I wouldn't have changed it for anything!"

If, on some far-distant day, her children asked her what she really missed the most during the busy, glamour-filled years, she said that, in full honesty, she could tell them, "Darling children, only the mumps."

Early on, she had a crush on Gary Cooper and thought Jimmy Dunn "dreamy"; she thought him even dreamier when he would smuggle ice cream to her on the set, disregarding her strictly supervised diet. She and Bill Robinson, the great black tap dancer, hit it off wonderfully well. She was teased by Arthur Treacher and retaliated in kind, once insisting that he move into a stall on the set and pretend to be a horse; he obliged and even neighed for her on cue when she brought people to visit him.

But it was Will Rogers who was her best friend. Says Jack Lait, then a Hearst writer and editor, "Will would talk Shirley's language, not baby talk and not shop. He had the heart of a child and he would make her giggle and she would call him Uncle Will. Will Rogers was the only actor the management allowed her to become chummy with."

Profile at Ten

When Rogers was killed in a plane crash in 1935, 20th Century dedicated a sound stage to his memory on the lot. After many celebrities had made their speeches, Shirley unveiled the bronze plaque they had put up at the entrance. All she said was, "I loved him, too."

At home, Shirley had a few selected playmates, all of whom had to come to her house and grounds. At Santa Monica, when she was taken to the beach, she was instantly recognized and surrounded. The Temples soon stopped that. Mary Lou Islieb, her studio stand-in, would be asked over often, and a fourteen-year-old boy who lived in the adjoining house would bring his pony and cart.

She accepted her role as America's princess without complaining about the restrictions it imposed on her freedoms. In her tenth year a reporter asked her, "Shirley, don't you ever get tired of people pushing and shoving you and asking you questions and begging for your autograph?"

"No," she answered. "I don't mind at all. It's part of the job."

Studio officials sought to create the impression that she was as unspoiled and well-behaved as the characters she portrayed in her movies. This was not always the case. She could be demanding and bossy, with adults as well as with other children. And, despite the official insistence that she was unaware of her great renown, she knew ever since she was six that she was a Movie Star.

On his first trip to the West Coast, André Sennwald, the young film critic of *The New York Times,* accepted the studio line as gospel, but the truth came to him crushingly, almost literally so, in the lobby of a theater in Santa Barbara where *Curly Top* was being previewed in 1935. Sennwald narrowly escaped serious harm when what he described as "an hysterical crowd" rushed out of the movie house.

"I leaped hastily behind a pillar to avoid being trampled," he said, "and, peering cautiously into the lobby to discover the cause of all the excitement, discovered little Shirley in the center of the stampede."

It is not likely that Shirley, even at seven, would think that such adulation is accorded to every little girl. Or that other nine-year-old children walk on a carpet of red plush as fans scream from behind police barricades, to be handed a magnificent bunch of red roses from Tyrone Power—as when *Wee Willie Winkie* had its world premiere. The evening she received her special Oscar, she sat at her table and said over and over to anybody who would listen, "When are they going to surprise me?" "Certainly she was aware she was a star," says Gene Reynolds. "How on earth could she help but know it?"

Diana Cary (Baby Peggy) relates the story of an interview Gertrude was giving a reporter about Shirley's daily activities. The little girl stood by listening for a time, then interrupted impatiently: "Why don't you interview me? I'm the star."

By the end of 1934, she was already going to the projection room when shooting ended to view the daily rushes and was asking to have the movie reviews read to her. She acceded to interviews graciously but, as time went on, became impatient with them. "They all ask you the same questions," she complained. "Like what is your favorite color, and what is your ambition."

One day, a fan magazine sent a photographer to the set for a picture layout. Shirley sat quietly where she was placed, then began fidgeting, as the cameraman was taking a long time to get his lights adjusted properly. Finally she spoke up: "Make the pictures now or not at all. I can't wait for you!"

Years later, she looked back and wondered how people could have put up with her.

Louis Sobol, a Broadway and Hollywood columnist for decades, says that after she was grown Shirley recognized that she had been "insufferable" as a child and was able to laugh about it. Sobol, eighty-five years old and living near the Times Square he wrote about from the twenties to the sixties, recalls an episode:

"I was in Hollywood, having lunch with Darryl Zanuck and Harry Brand, the publicity chief, and a couple of others. Zanuck said, 'Oh, by the way, I want you to meet this marvelous star we have. Would you like to meet her?'

"I said, 'Sure,' so he whispers something into Harry's ear and he leaves. Well, we go on with our lunch and before we finish Harry comes back, and with him is this little six-year-old and her mother. Darryl says to her, 'Honey, this is one of the big newspapermen from New York, and he came out here especially to see you. Now, isn't that nice?'

"She just looked at him and smiled, and he said, 'I think it would be very nice if you sat on his lap and took a picture with him. Wouldn't that be nice?' She said nothing, just looked at him, and her mother said, 'Now, honey, you know what to do. This man came all the way from New York to see you.'

"So she sat on my lap, cuddly and lovely. The minute the cameraman was through, she jumped off, gave me a disdainful look and started to run off. Her mother grabbed her and said, 'Where are you going?' Shirley said, 'Why do you make me do silly things like this?' And she gave me another disdainful look.

"Years passed, and I'm in the Stork Club and in comes this good-looking dame. At that time she must have been about twenty-five. Sherman [Sherman Billingsley, the club's owner] comes over to me and says, 'Do you know who that is?'

"I told him the face looks familiar but I couldn't place it. He said, 'That's Shirley Temple.' So I went over to her and I told her about the episode, and she says, 'I was really something in those days, wasn't I? I don't know why anybody tolerated me. I had an ego. But they helped it along.'"

Sobol's longtime colleague Sidney Skolsky is probably the only person besides her mother ever to spank Shirley Temple. She gave him good reason. Skolsky, who has written about Hollywood and its personalities since the early 1930s, still has an office in Schwab's Pharmacy on Sunset Boulevard, where he tells the hilarious tale of upending Shirley for bratty behavior and the consequences thereof:

"It was my first year on my Hollywood assignment and I wasn't accustomed to the bright sunshine. I broke out in a rash whenever I was exposed to its rays. I went to doctors in Los Angeles, but they couldn't tell me what was wrong, so when I returned to New York on my vacation I went to see my old physician. He told me that I was allergic to the sun and that I should wear a hat to shield my face and forehead. I'd never worn one before, but it was doctor's orders, so I bought a nice felt one.

"One day, when I visited Fox on my rounds, I put the hat on a desk in the publicity department. Shirley was there, visiting with her mother as she often did. She took my hat from the desk and threw it on the floor. I picked it up and she threw it down again. After she had done it a third time, I told her, 'Shirley, that's my hat and you shouldn't do that.' Whereupon, just for spite, she took the hat and threw it on the floor again.

"Well, that did it. I picked her up, put her across my knees and started spanking her.

"It was like a signal. Within two minutes it seemed that every executive and assistant at Fox was in the office making me stop. I haven't the faintest idea how they knew their meal ticket was being spanked, but apparently someone in publicity called the executive floor. Shirley never cried, just yelled one time, 'Hey, that hurts!'

"After that, she behaved herself. Later, to show there was peace between us, she let me escort her to the preview of one of her films at Grauman's Chinese. She behaved like a little lady. She didn't think much of the picture. When it was over, we walked out and I delivered her to her mother, and that was the end of my date. From then on, we got along fine."

A Talk with Her Director

At ninety-six, Allan Dwan called himself the oldest living motion picture pioneer. Toronto-born, he began his film career the year after D. W. Griffith and, over the years, directed, produced and supervised some eight hundred pictures. He worked with Mary Pickford, the Gish girls, Douglas Fairbanks—and Shirley Temple.

In the living room of his white stucco cottage in Van Nuys, he talks about the little girl he directed in *Heidi* (1937), *Rebecca of Sunnybrook Farm* (1938) and *Young People* (1940).

Allan Dwan: "Often her mother didn't think Shirley was listening to my directions. So she would speak to her, tell her to pay more careful attention. Then Shirley would pick out another little girl in the cast and say the same thing to her, bawl her out for not being attentive. The little girl would look at her with great big eyes and start to cry, thinking she'd done something wrong. That would make things even worse for the kid. Because then Mrs. Temple would take her aside and bawl her out again, this time for making Shirley unhappy.

"The funny part is that while Shirley gave the impression of not being attentive, she heard everything and, with that fabulous memory, could rattle off verbatim everything she was told.

"When she heard me tell the electricians to put a spotlight up or take one down, she would choose a little girl, tell her where to sit or stand and then call up to the lighting man. Imitating my voice, and using my words, she would issue the same orders. The little girl would be baffled and the electricians were convulsed.

"She did things like that so frequently, I'd have to rap for her to be quiet. Then she'd imitate my raps and turn to the other kids—who hadn't been making any noise—and whisper, 'Sh-h.'

"She decided that she wanted to take charge of the children in the cast. In *Heidi*, we had a lot of kids dressed as little Dutch girls doing a folk dance. One of the steps, a fairly intricate one, called for them to place one leg over the other. Many of them became confused and got it all wrong and would even fall down trying to do it. Shirley would bawl them out and say, 'Look, you do it this way.' They would argue back and forth. She was stubborn and would say, 'No, it's *this* way,' and show them again. Well, the dancing master finally got them all together and straightened them out.

"Since she obviously wanted to take charge, I figured out a way to let her do it constructively. I had a bunch of little badges made, with SHIRLEY TEMPLE POLICE stamped on them. Every kid who came on the set had to wear a badge and join the force and swear allegiance to Shirley, guaranteeing to obey her. Pretty soon, we had almost everyone on the set wearing a badge, with Shirley sporting one labeled CHIEF.

"Those badges carried a lot more weight than I expected. One morning I got a late start and was driving too fast to the studio. A cop pulled me over and, not at all friendly, let me know that I was exceeding the speed limit. As he was reaching for his book, I began explaining I was in a hurry to get to the studio because I was a film director and that my star was waiting for me with a big company, and I should have been there ten minutes ago.

"I could see he didn't believe a word, especially the way I was dressed. In those days you put on your worst clothes because they'd all be ruined on the set. 'What's this bum trying to give me?' he was probably thinking. I guess I even looked as though I had stolen the car I was driving.

"I thought fast. I pulled out my badge which said SHIRLEY TEMPLE POLICE and flashed it. He stared at it, and said, 'Holy So-and-So! My kid would give her right arm for this.' I pushed it on him. 'Here,' I said, 'take it, give it to her with Shirley's compliments.' He pinned it right under his own official LAPD badge and waved me on. No ticket, of course.

"That badge was useful lots of other ways. When I went into a restaurant or night club without a reservation, I'd pull it out and the headwaiter would get me the best table in the house. It happened all the time.

"We even issued official documents with the badge, attesting to the fact that the wearer belonged to the 'department.' It began to backfire a little. Shirley took it so seriously she said no child who was not a member of the corps could work in a picture. She made it a closed shop, so we signed up every kid we hired.

"She was a little big shot and loved it. If I had to leave the set, I'd tell her, 'Shirley, now you take charge of things.' And she did. She strutted around giving orders, like 'I want you to take that set down and put up a castle.' The grips would pretend to carry out the instructions, satisfying her, going along with the game.

"Once her parents gave her a set of drums, which she brought to the studio. She set them up on the set, next to the drummer for the band which played for the musical numbers, and he taught her how to play them. The trouble was we couldn't get her to stop. Even her mother had her hands full trying to keep her from banging away when she shouldn't.

"She organized an orchestra. She got a lot of kids with fake violins and other instruments to stand up and solo away while she hit the drums. This racket would prevail through the set and into other sets until complaints would come in: 'Hey, stop that music over there for a while so we can catch a shot, will you!'"

David Butler, who directed Shirley in five films, was impressed by her total professionalism, and absolute fearlessness, on the set. She did as she was told, despite the risks. A case in point was the time a crane bit down hard on her nose and refused to let go. It happened during the filming of *Captain January,* with Buddy Ebsen, Guy Kibbee and Slim Summerville, a movie which represented the peak of the Temple years.

Butler: "The one story that I remember about *Captain January:* Sheehan was a man who would look at the newsreel, or he'd see something somewhere in a show, and he'd call the directors in and say, 'I saw this, and try and fit it in the picture.' When this picture was going on, he had seen a newsreel of a crane with a big beak, and he wanted to fit it into *Captain January* some way. There was a crane that was down at the zoo, and it did certain tricks. So somebody thought of the idea of having Shirley's birthday, and they were going to give her the crane as a gift, and put a big bow on it. So Slim Summerville, who was in the picture, was Captain January's friend. And he was going to lead the crane. So we got to the picture, and Slim Summerville has a rope around the crane's neck, and leads it into the picture. He whistles for Shirley, and she looks out from the top of the lighthouse. We got a shot of her running down the stairs. When she got down he said, 'Happy birthday. This is for you.' And Shirley said, 'For *me?*' And with that the crane reached out and grabbed hold of her nose, and took a tight hold of her nose. We couldn't get it to release its bill. It still hung on. We had an awful time. They had to chloroform the crane to release Shirley's nose."

If Shirley helped Allan Dwan with his problems on the set, she was equally ready to offer her services to Butler. In *Bright Eyes,* the director had difficulties with Jane Withers, who would silently mouth the lines spoken by Shirley in their scenes. Butler would stop the camera, take Jane aside and say, "Jane, you mouthed what Shirley is going to say, and you can see it on your lips."

"'Oh,' she said, 'I'm sorry. I won't do it again.' Then I felt a little tug on my sleeve. It was Shirley. She beckoned to me, and she said, whispering, 'I'll watch her, and if she does it and you can't see it, I'll shake my head like this. But if she's all right, I'll give you the nod this way.' So I said, 'All right, Shirley.' We had our secret. And, by golly, she did it. If Jane mouthed, she'd go like this, shake her head, and I'd cut. And when she finally got it all right, Shirley was so proud. She nodded that everything was all right."

Butler and Shirley had another problem with a child actor that neither was able to solve quite so easily. The script of *The Little Colonel* called for a scene in which Shirley baptized a little black youngster in a river. After a series of auditions, Butler chose an adorable child named Junior who, despite his charm and appeal, didn't know much if anything about taking direction.

Butler: "He was a wild man. We had an awful time even keeping him in a scene, to walk down a set. He'd be looking all around or fooling with his pants. But we managed to get by with it after working quite hard. And Junior was there and he was cute on the screen, the little guy.

"So now we came to the baptism, where Shirley has to dunk him under in the water, and she says, 'Are you saved?' And he has to shake his head and say, 'No,' and she dunks him again. So we'd get him all set, and the cameras and so forth. And Shirley would dunk him down under. 'Are you saved?' He'd come up and shake his head. Then he'd grab Shirley and duck *her* under!

"Well, I want to tell you that I was ready to kill that kid. We changed her clothes. We fixed her makeup at least five times. Every time we'd do it he'd shove her in the water. So finally his mother told him she was going to give him a good spanking if he did it again, so we finally got the scene. But this was after changing Shirley five times. He'd grab her and duck her and hold her under, and the whole crew would jump in to save Shirley. When we finished, I told his mother, 'I'll tell you something about Junior. He's going to be fine in the picture, but he caused me a lot of trouble. And I'll bet you he winds up a porter on the train.'

"Now twenty years elapsed, and I'm going to New York on the Chief. I got in my compartment, and in comes a porter. He says,

'Mr. Butler, you don't remember me, do you?' I said, 'No.' And it was Junior! He did wind up a porter. It was so funny. And then we sat down and talked about it. He looked just the same except older. But that face he had—that was a funny, funny thing."

Cast and crew worked hard during the making of a picture, and, to ease the tensions, parties were frequent. Birthdays were always a good excuse, especially Shirley's. On these occasions, directors and screenwriters worked for days, planning divertissements. Once Butler was host at a party at the Beverly Hills Country Club, to which he invited the entire company. He helped devise a trick he would remember years later.

"When her birthday cake came out," he said, "we turned out all the lights. Shirley was at the head of the table. Out from the kitchen came this chef with his white hat on. He walked toward Shirley, and as he got near her he tripped, and his face went right into the cake."

Shirley, of course, howled, but it had all been faked. A stunt man named Sailor Vincent had been hired to plop his face into the whipped cream. Afterward, the real cake was brought out.

Shirley's success was compounded of a variety of factors, not the least of which was a true talent which in almost no time at all had developed into thoroughgoing professionalism.

As early as age five, she had astonished—and dismayed—fellow actors, who as a general rule do not suffer excellence in their co-stars gladly. After the first morning's shooting of *Little Miss Marker*, Adolphe Menjou, one of Hollywood's most adroit scene-stealers, arrived at the Fox commissary for lunch looking as sorrowful as the character he was portraying, a gambler named Sorrowful Jones. "I want to quit," he announced to his companions. "That Temple kid, she scares me."

So upset he was unable to eat, Menjou said he had played with many actresses and learned a bagful of tricks to defend himself against those who would take scenes from him. "But this child frightens me," he said. "She knows all the tricks." He ticked them off: Shirley would move forward, forcing him to back out of camera range; Shirley would "step" on his lines; Shirley would do something that would abort his laughs. "She's making a stooge out of me," he complained. "Why, if she were forty years old and on the stage all her life, she wouldn't have had time to learn all that she knows about acting. Don't ask me how she does it. You've heard of chess champions at eight and violin virtuosos at ten? Well, she's an Ethel Barrymore at four."

Shirley won him over by the end of the next week. An assistant director who went looking for him found him playing jacks with her on her dressing-room floor.

Two years later, during the making of *Dimples*, the story of a Bowery waif who becomes the toast of Broadway, Frank Morgan said, "she is the greatest actress I ever played with."

Lionel Barrymore, his tantrum over her prompting ended, felt her talent was "God-given" and compared her to his grandmother, Louisa Drew, a child prodigy at six who astonished critics with her versatility and was also received by a President, Andrew Jackson. During the filming of *The Little Colonel*, Shirley would whisper to him her own interpretation of the scene they were doing and the motivations of the characters; her reasoning, Barrymore said, was done "with rare intelligence in her own manner."

Before the picture was finished, she had won him over completely. On the last day of shooting, he was putting on his makeup when he felt a tug at his sleeve. Looking down, he saw Shirley extending her autograph book. "Can I have your autograph, Uncle Lionel?" she asked. Tears welled in his eyes, recalls David Butler. "He grabbed hold of her and kissed her and it was just a great moment. He cried like a baby, after going through everything with this kid. When she left, he said, 'You were right, David. That was a great experience. I wouldn't have missed it for the world.'"

Shirley's abundant charm endeared her to moviegoers. "But there were many other kids just as pretty or prettier," says Allan Dwan, "and we had to be very careful in casting a movie to weed those out. They'd detract from Shirley.

"People came to see Shirley because of those dimples and her cuteness," he pointed out. "Many failed to realize, and I'm sure many still may be surprised to discover, that she was a superbly talented actress."

This was recognized not only by her colleagues but by scholarly critics, newspaper reviewers and the shrewdly observant bible of show business, *Variety*. In 1937, Gilbert Seldes, a distinguished commentator on American entertainment arts, wrote: "I am sure that a thousand people went to see Shirley Temple because she was 'cute' for every hundred who went because she was, at least in her early pictures, quite a remarkable actress. Not to acknowledge this is to be both a fanatic and a fool . . ." Sennwald of *The New York Times* hailed her "remarkable sense of timing" and the assurance and precision of her dramatic scenes in *The Little Colonel* (1935). The *New York World-Telegram* called her "one of the most amazing actresses in Hollywood"; to the *New York Daily News* she was "charming and unaffected"; and to *Variety* she was "a great little artist." In Hollywood it is a given fact that the hardest people to impress with performances are the technicians. Shirley even won the applause of her cameraman, Arthur C. Miller, who worked with nearly every important producer, director and actor in the business from 1922 until his retirement in the 1950s. Miller, who filmed most of the Temple pictures at Fox and 20th Century, declared in 1967, "I don't believe there ever will be another child actress with her exceptional talent."

And Bosley Crowther, reviewing her performance in *Rebecca of Sunnybrook Farm* in the *Times,* committed to print and posterity this astonishing statement:

> We are quite serious about this: any actress who can dominate a Zanuck musical . . . with Jack Haley, Gloria Stuart, Phyllis Brooks, Helen Westley, Slim Summerville, Bill Robinson, et cetera, can dominate the world. We go even further: we venture to predict for Miss Temple a great future, and that includes singing, dancing, straight dramatic acting, or all three combined, if her fancy runs that way. When it comes to sheer histrionism, we consider her greater than Garbo, Luise Rainer, Hepburn, the Barrymore family (its heirs and assigns), Ginger Rogers and Gypsy Rose—pardon us—Louise Hovick. And Shirley will get you, too, if you don't watch out.

Crowther's tongue may have been jutting deeply into his cheek, but he continued in subsequent notices to call her a "miracle child." But no matter; she *was* good. Allan Dwan recalls that she was excellent at portraying anger. "She could get so mad," he said, "she'd tear the set down. There was probably a good deal of suppressed anger in her, and acting gave her a chance to express herself. I believe she was dying to do something tragic, or dramatic. Here's how we got her to show anger when the scenes called for it: I'd say to her at the start, 'Now, Shirley, you're mad, very, very mad.' Then she would start to growl and I would growl back at her a little louder. Then she'd top me and I'd growl louder still until we were both snarling at each other like mad dogs. We'd shoot the scene and the sparks would fly."

Lyle Talbot, who acted with her in *Our Little Girl*, described a scene in which she erupts in anger at him: "There was something heartbreaking in the emotion she displayed—half rage, half childish dismay. She made the scene so real with her little eyes flashing and her baby's voice breaking with rage, that the entire troupe was impressed, and very quiet when the scene was finished."

In all her movies, Shirley's tears were real. Her directors never resorted to chemicals that irritate the tear ducts, such as glycerine and tincture of menthol. They did, however, use tricks.

Allan Dwan: "Every director uses tricks with children. But you've got to be very careful, because after you get a kid crying he or she doesn't forget so easily. They feel so badly they'll worry about it all night or even longer. Then their parents will call you and ask, 'Why did you scare my kid?'

"Shirley didn't cry easily. We had to use tricks with her too, keep inventing gags of one kind or another. Because she was blessed with a pretty good appetite, a simple one worked well. We'd tell her she couldn't have lunch that day. On hearing this, she'd start wailing. Then, when we had the scene and enough tears, we'd have another problem—how to get her to stop. We'd send somebody out quickly, or have the lunch all ready, and she'd quiet down.

"When she got a little older, the lunch thing didn't work any more, so I'd take her aside and tell her, 'Now, Shirley, I want you to think that you'll never see your mother again. Think hard, she's gone, gone for good. She'll never, never, never come back.' I'd go on like that and pretty soon the tears would boil out of her."

In *Little Miss Marker*, director Alexander Hall put on a long face and told Shirley that the brand-new red car the Temples had acquired had been in a wreck, and that her mother had gone off to see about the damage. Shirley burst into tears. As she grew older, she no longer needed outside help to weep. She brought on tears by herself, quietly and professionally.

Cameraman Miller: "Shirley would think how terrible it would be if her little Pekingese Ming Toy were hurt. Shirley's method was no secret. The whole crew knew it and would go on with their work as quietly as possible. At this moment Shirley was treated as an adult. When she felt she was ready to cry and sob, she would deliberately walk to her position where the scene had been rehearsed, and usually two cameras, one medium and the closeup, would roll and the scene would be shot. In a few minutes of standing on the sidelines by herself after the scene was finished, Shirley reverted to her usual cheerful disposition."

She was never an exceptional singer. "Her voice," says Dwan, "was just a noise that came out of her. Like a little doll. If the music was loud and we had a choral group behind her, it was easy to do. Or is she was singing with Bill Robinson or somebody else, then, yes, it would be good. If she did it alone, it was too much tempo. No originality, no variation."

Her dancing, however, was something else. "She had something that is very rare," Dwan declares, "a sense of balance and of rhythm. Her dancing was done with no sense of strain, she exhibited a considerable skill and a frankly phenomenal ability to absorb steps of great intricacy."

From Bill Robinson, the legendary Bojangles who was one of the greatest tap dancers show business ever produced, she had learned five complete routines for *The Little Colonel* in a single morning—three tap, one waltz clog and a soft-shoe. Not once as he danced for her in a rehearsal room did she ever look at his feet; she just listened to them and memorized the steps. Toward noon, when they were finished, Robinson wept and kissed both her feet, saying, "Uncle Bill doesn't tell her feet where to go. Her heart tells her."

Director David Butler recalls that a day or so later, when they would rehearse the steps before the scene was to be shot, Robinson would have to stop and think about what came next. Shirley, remembering perfectly, would tell the master, "Oh, here's what we've got to do here, Uncle Bill."

Only once did the studio have to resort to fakery. *Poor Little Rich Girl* concludes with a lengthy sequence, danced to the tune of "I Love a Military Man," which she does with Jack Haley and Alice Faye. Her taps didn't satisfy the director, who ordered new ones dubbed in, Haley later revealed. However, neither Shirley nor her mother was told. At the preview, Gertrude beamed and said, "Did you hear those taps? Could they have been any clearer?" Still, the number has won high praise from critics and film historians. William K. Everson, professor of cinema at New York University, points out, "The sequence goes on for minutes at a time without any need to cut away from Shirley, which means that she was able to memorize that long, very complicated routine. The number, which runs more than five minutes, was done in no more than three takes, unique for a dancer, remarkable for a little girl."

Overlaying her natural talent and developing skills was an appeal that has defied even partially satisfactory definition and remains a tantalizing mystery still. The magnetism that Shirley had, possessed by all other successful screen personalities, has been variously described as "magic," "star quality," "charisma" and, by Rudy Vallee, as "I'll be darned if I know or if anybody else does, either."

Vallee, eighty-one years old in 1982, still travels around the country performing a routine he created, involving slides and songs, acted with Shirley in *The Bachelor and the Bobby Soxer* in 1947. He says, "What did this kid have that made her famous? What did Chevalier have? He couldn't sing worth a god-damn, he wasn't especially handsome, with his capped teeth—yet he had an incredible appeal that made him a great success on screen and with the women off screen. Bottle it and you could make the world's biggest fortune. No matter what Shirley did, she could do no wrong. She had that grand quality that reached out at the audience and held it."

None of Shirley's directors, those still living and the ones who left their recollections, has been able to define any more accurately that rare quality communicated between performer and audience. After forty-five years in Hollywood, Skolsky admits that an explanation still eludes him.

The special human components that make up stardom came together in Shirley Temple, but the parts remain nature's secret. Until it is unlocked, if it ever is, moviegoers must believe, with Keats, that that is all they know on earth and all they need to know.

Still, even talent and appeal were not all. They flocked to see Shirley because she conveyed the reassurance that purity and innocence, which she represented, could solve the problems and the despairs of people's lives, that incorruptible good and spunky self-reliance can triumph over any evil.

She fixed things up in sixty-four minutes, her shortest film (*Our Little Girl*, 1935), to 105 minutes, her longest (*Wee Willie Winkie*, 1937). Within these time spans, she turned crusty curmudgeons into sweet old gentlemen by discovering the warm heart beneath the icy exterior; she was a Cupid who brought warring lovers and wives and husbands together; she reunited parents estranged from their children; she transformed an empty cheerless mansion of a wealthy man into a happy home filled with laughter and people; she showed neglectful fathers, skinflint tycoons, malevolent lawmen and sourpuss dowagers the error of their ways.

She was never sticky-sweet about any of this. Rather, she was a peppery little miss, sometimes a little sassy, who refused to be cowed by powerful people or adversity, a trait characteristic of pioneer women which has always been admired. That it should be exhibited by a little girl was all the more impressive. Filmgoers beaten down by the world's pressures in those bleak days took heart by watching Shirley stand up to authority, whether it was a thin-lipped, cruel owner of a school for young ladies, bad men who sought to rob her father of the deed to a railroad or a rebeling amir in the Khyber Pass.

103

The final scene in *Heidi* (1937) is quintessential Temple: Heidi has been reunited with her aged grandfather and is living with him in his mountain home. Up the hill comes Clara, once wheelchair-bound and now running, thanks to Shirley's therapeutic pep talks, followed by a puffing Herr Sesemann, Clara's father.

Lunch is served outdoors in a clearing at a table set among tall trees. As grace is being said, the camera moves in on Shirley who, with eyes closed, says, "And please make every little boy and girl in the world as happy as I am."

She opens her eyes, smiles radiantly straight into the camera and into the hearts of audiences everywhere, who exit from the movie theater with their own smiles, perhaps the suspicion of tears behind the eyes, and, most of all, feeling good.

It was a very good year, her tenth. The reviews for her *Rebecca of Sunnybrook Farm* were close to rapturous, the cheerleading led by *Variety*: "Shirley Temple proves she's a great little artist in this one. The national No. 1 star seldom has shown so brilliantly in her singing, dancing and repartee. That means she's going right ahead to bigger and better grosses." The *World-Telegram* wrote that "the little star has never been more engaging and captivating."

Rebecca was followed by *Just Around the Corner* and *Little Miss Broadway*, both formula Temple, each making money. Darryl Zanuck as he counted the receipts crowed gleefully that Shirley would be "good for years." After all, wasn't she still number-one box-office leader?

Zanuck guessed wrong. By 1939, after one last big blip with *The Little Princess*, Shirley slid to number-five on the box-office list, and from that time she skidded rapidly down.

Part Two
GROWING UP

9

Schoolgirl

The magical years had come to an end.

In January of 1940, 20th Century–Fox released *The Blue Bird*, but it failed to fly. Maurice Maeterlinck's fantasy of the woodsman's daughter who pursues the legendary bird in a dream world expired at the box office, though Shirley got high marks for her portrayal of Mytyl. It was a $2-million flop, her first failure. Out of Zanuck's earshot, studio wags pronounced it a dead pigeon, and with it went the incredible Temple era.

Later that year, *Young People* came into the theaters, and moviegoers saw a twelve-year-old, four-foot-nine-inch Shirley, no longer the enchanting child and not yet a winsome teenager. *Young People* was a sentimental fable about a couple of retired vaudeville troupers and their daughter who go to live in a stuffy New England town. The movie stressed heavily the joys of retirement, which should have alerted the Temples to what was coming. Equally ominous for the dying legend was the coolness of audiences, which gave it the smattering of applause usually accorded next-to-closing acts. The *Times* said it best when it referred to Shirley as a "superannuated sunbeam."

Reports circulated in Hollywood that it was all Gertrude's fault.

She countercharged that poor scripts and not she or Shirley were to blame. "I wasn't the heavy," she insisted. "It has been said that I was responsible for the selection of Shirley's stories. But that wasn't so. I've never had anything to say about her pictures, their stories, their casts and I still don't. It has hurt to read that I personally was responsible for her films being bad."

The Temples exercised their option to buy up Shirley's contract for a reputed $300,000; 20th Century–Fox made no objections and gave Shirley a farewell party. The company was downright niggardly in its goodbye gifts to the little girl who had saved it from collapse, presenting her with the upright piano from her cottage and an assortment of costumes she had worn. Jack Oakie, who played her ex-trouper father in *Young People*, was disgusted. "The kid who had coined millions for the industry received a chill from the studio to go down in movie history," he said.

Shirley's future might have taken a wholly different turn if Louis B. Mayer and Nicholas Schenck, the ruling powers at Metro-Goldwyn-Mayer Studios, had been able to pry her loose from Zanuck. Both had wanted to cast her in the role of Dorothy in *The Wizard of Oz*.

Mayer was unimpressed with Judy Garland, whose candidacy for the part was being promoted by Mervyn LeRoy and Arthur Freed. Contemptuously, he referred to her as "that big-assed kid." Zanuck, however, had repeatedly rebuffed his pleas to borrow Shirley, the proven money-maker. Finally Mayer gave up, LeRoy and Freed got their way, and Judy's performance became a movie legend.

Still, it is interesting to conjecture about what the outcome would have been if Shirley had been tagged. While she was far behind Judy in vocal ability, she radiated charm and would have been a more authentic Dorothy because she was closer to the age that L. Frank Baum envisaged for his heroine. Dorothy, Baum wrote, "had been a little girl when she first came to the Land of Oz . . . and would never seem to be a day older while she lived in this wonderful fairyland." Moreover, the illustrations for the original Oz books by William Wallace Denslow pictured Dorothy as a young child. Judy was fifteen; her enlarging bosom had to be strapped tightly to make her appear prepubescent.

Back home, Gertrude and George decided it was time to broaden their daughter's educational horizons. She was still being tutored, and Gertrude felt a change was imperative. She said, "I don't want Shirley to say to me, 'Mother, why couldn't I have gone to school just like any other girl?'"

In September of 1940, with *Young People* still playing to sparse audiences, the Temples enrolled her at the Westlake School for Girls, a fashionable institution which occupied an eleven-acre estate in Holmby Hills, adjacent to Bel-Air and Beverly Hills. Daughters of affluent and prominent families were students at the school, which ranked with such swank Eastern establishments as Miss Hewitt's in New York and Miss Porter's in Connecticut. Myrna Loy had attended Westlake; Harold Lloyd's daughters, Gloria and Peggy, and Spencer Tracy's Susie were also Westlake girls. The school had an enrollment of only 250 and a curriculum that laid heavy emphasis on culture: liberal arts, languages, music and drama. Some of the graduates went on to college; for many, however, a Westlake education ended their schooldays.

Westlake had been founded in 1904 by Frederica de Laguna and Jessica Smith Vance, teaching associates at the University of Southern California, who named it after Westlake Park, which was close to its original site. It had been at its present location at 700 North Faring Road since 1928. Students either boarded at the school or arrived each morning for classes, many in limousines.

While Shirley had turned a corner, she had not retired. She appeared that year in a series of original radio dramas, with co-stars like Warner Baxter, Robert Young, Lionel Barrymore and Humphrey Bogart, which she described as "a big thrill." She also played the lead in *Junior Miss,* a radio series based on the enormously popular Sally Benson stories in *The New Yorker,* detailing the adventures of a young woman just about Shirley's age.

Metro-Goldwyn-Mayer signed her for two pictures. The first, *Kathleen,* was to be released in 1941, and Shirley was delighted because it was a grown-up role and she could wear a long dress and be glamorous. Her co-stars in *Kathleen,* a saccharine story of a motherless girl, her indifferent father and the psychologist who makes everything come out all right (an inevitable ending for a Shirley Temple movie) were Herbert Marshall, Laraine Day and Gail Patrick.

The reviews were poor, with the *New York Times* critic declaring: "MGM, her new sponsors, haven't done right by Shirley. Out of her indubitable charm, they have created a vexatious, pucker-faced little brat full of raging day dreams to make an audience wince. . . . Miss Temple tries hard," he notes, but "they have confronted her proven talents as an actress with stilted situations that even a Duse couldn't carry off."

The Temples and MGM agreed to forget the whole thing, and a few months later Shirley signed a contract with Edward Small for *Miss Annie Rooney,* co-starring her partner of Baby Burlesk days, Dickie Moore. The two did some fast dancing and used lots of teenage slang, and he gingerly planted a highly publicized "first screen kiss" on her left cheek as he drove to a party at his Sutton Place mansion.

Its release led William Boehnel of the *New York World-Telegram* to say that "recently Miss Temple [had] had some pretty feeble material but none so commonplace as this." The *New York Times* critic called it a "very grim little picture."

> *Miss Annie Rooney* [that same critic said] is the kind of show that makes indulgent souls feel much less kind toward children. If 14-year-olds must pass through the pains of puppy love, must indulge in swivel-jointed kiddie capers, or if they must travel about in a weary old scrap-heap called Ana-esthesia, Mr. Small—whose vehicle for Miss Temple is closely comparable to the above mentioned conveyance—has done nothing to prove that these pastimes should not be strictly private. . . . Meanwhile, couldn't Miss Temple be kept in school for just a little while?

Apparently his advice was taken. No more picture deals were announced and Shirley concentrated on her studies.

She had entered Westlake in the seventh grade. Classes had already begun for the fall term when the chauffeur drove Shirley and Mrs. Temple through the black wrought-iron gate onto the beautifully landscaped grounds. Several girls, wearing the school's smartly tailored blue uniform, lounged near the canopied entrance to the main building.

Shirley eyed them curiously and wondered whether she would fit in. She had never been part of a social group and she looked forward to the experience. Gertrude was thinking hard, too. Since Shirley's birth, they had been together constantly. She had supervised every moment of Shirley's day, made all her decisions. How would Shirley do on her own? And how would she, Gertrude, fare without Shirley?

Mother and daughter got out of the car and looked at the two-story beige stucco building, its red tile roof and arched windows typical of the Spanish-influenced architecture of California. Tall observation towers rose from the roof, and a stone wall surrounded the handsome campus, which was crossed by paved walks interspersed with lush plantings.

They went through the great hall, with its polished wood floor, pillars and arches and into the office, where Mrs. Temple introduced Shirley to Carol Mills, the principal, and repeated her request that Shirley be treated like any other student.

It was not that easy. In the next few weeks, Shirley met with hostility for probably the first time in her life. Convinced that her movie stardom must have filled her with exaggerated notions of her worth, some of the girls decided to humble her. "That first week," she recalled later, "one of the students, a very sophisticated girl and very much the leader of social activities, startled me by inviting every girl in the group to a party except me. I was not hurt, just surprised—surprised to learn that being Shirley Temple didn't solve everything."

The tensions eased and Shirley began to enjoy herself. "In two weeks I learned more from the students than I had discovered in all my five years of private tutoring," she says. "There was so much to look at and listen to—the whispering, the gossip and all the wonderful things that young girls do. I learned about the new hairdos and how to pass personal notes without their being intercepted."

She also learned a few things which Gertrude hadn't counted on.

While Shirley's preparation for Westlake was thorough enough in academic subjects, she was less equipped in other areas. Sheltered as she had been by the studio from vulgarity and profanity unsuitable for a little girl, she knew few dirty and no off-color stories, a deficiency in her education which her classmates soon discovered and set about to remedy.

Soon after she arrived, they taught her a ribald story and a smutty poem. At the dinner table at home one evening, when Gertrude asked Shirley the customary parental question, "And what did you learn in school today?" her daughter, beaming, told the joke and recited the poem. Needless to say, she understood neither. Dead silence followed. Gertrude and George looked at each other and then Mrs. Temple sighed and told her daughter that those were not the sort of things she should be repeating.

Shirley conformed to the Westlake mold, wore the regulation uniform, low-heeled shoes, no makeup or jewelry. She went to parties with her classmates and dances at a local military school. She was a great dancer and an extremely popular partner. At one dance, she was cut in on thirty times. She was not, as yet, allowed unchaperoned dates.

Shirley had small parts in some of the school's dramatic shows, never trying for leads because, she explained, she had only movie and no stage experience. At freshman hazing, given the task of singing "Baby, Take a Bow," in the same manner as in the movie, she demurred. "I honestly can't remember," she explained. "Besides, I never watched Shirley work. Won't you show me how she did it?"

She went to the movies with her parents and clothes-shopping with Gertrude; she also served on various committees, including one which arranged blind dates for Westlake girls with students of the nearby boys' schools. Gertrude was active in the Westlake Mothers Club.

Although, in her early movie career days, press agents had

boasted that her IQ was 155, this did not show up in her grades, which were Bs and Cs. The fabulous memory which earned her the nickname One-Take Temple was no help scholastically. "Trouble is," she explained, "I learn things quickly, but I don't retain. In pictures I have to remember my lines perfectly, but I can forget them as soon as the scene is finished. So that's the way my mind works."

Gertrude, however, saw it somewhat differently. If Shirley would spend less time on the telephone each night and devote those hours to homework, undistracted by the radio which was constantly blaring, her marks would be higher, she said. Shirley's typically teenage response was, "I really do better with shrieks and eeks in my ear. It forms a kind of background and rests my mind when I work." Gertrude was about as successful as most mothers in eliminating the distractions.

In her French class one day, a visiting teacher was explaining how easy it was to learn the language. He started his talk with an anecdote about Adolphe Menjou and Shirley Temple. Almost imperceptibly the girls began to straighten up and lean forward, as if to catch every word.

Menjou had called Shirley, the teacher said, and asked how she was doing. "I'm not doing so well with my French," she told him, according to the teacher.

The teacher paused, somewhat disconcerted by the smiles which had begun to appear on the faces of the students. Then he continued.

"'I'll tell you how to double the French words you know in one minute,'" he quoted Menjou as saying to Shirley.

"'How?'

"'Well, Shirley, you see, every word that ends in *ion* is the same in French as it is in English.'"

By now the girls were shaking with laughter, and the hapless man was really confused. He had not recognized Shirley—sitting in the front row and laughing as hard as the others.

Charles Laughton didn't recognize her, either, the day he came to Westlake to give Shakespearean readings. They had met at a benefit for China Relief, and Shirley, awaiting her turn in the wings, had listened enthralled as he recited the Gettysburg Address.

At Westlake, Laughton sat in a great armchair, the girls gathered on the rug about him. He glanced curiously at Shirley and asked, "Don't I know you?"

Shirley, an incorrigible tease (a trait she had picked up from her father), was noncommittal. Laughton continued the readings, looking at her from time to time. When it was over, the giggling students solved the mystery and introduced them.

After a two-year absence from the screen, Shirley's career took off again in 1944 when David O. Selznick, who already had Ingrid Bergman, Jennifer Jones, Joan Fontaine and Joseph Cotten under contract, planned to present Shirley as a typical teenager, who would gradually mature before the eyes of the screen audiences.

Her first picture for Selznick was *Since You Went Away*, which showed how an American family coped on the home front. Shirley played Brig, the fifteen-year-old daughter of Claudette Colbert. She loved the role.

"Brig was a breeze," she said. "I knew all about her right from the beginning because she was me."

Selznick, however, did not want the film to be seen primarily as Shirley's picture and stressed this in a memo to Joseph Henry Steele, director of advertising and publicity, ordering that casting stories list Colbert first, Jones second, Monte Woolley third and Temple fourth. "I'm anxious to get the accent off this as a Temple vehicle," he wrote.

The critics accepted it that way. Colbert, and Jennifer Jones, who played Shirley's older sister, won the most plaudits, and the young Robert Walker (as a GI) was hailed as "uncommonly appealing" by the *Times*, which cast a little nosegay to Shirley, calling her "pert as the young sister."

Her next Selznick picture, *I'll Be Seeing You*, was also a World War II story, with Shirley playing the seventeen-year-old niece of Ginger Rogers and Joseph Cotten, a shellshocked apathetic veteran. Bosley Crowther, the *New York Times* critic, rated her performance "splendid."

Shirley turned sixteen while making *I'll Be Seeing You* and celebrated with an ice-cream-and-cake party on the set, festive enough but a far cry from the extravaganzas hosted by Fox in her earlier days. Most of her presents were the gag variety: Ginger Rogers presented her with a John Fredericks hat of chicken feathers, Cotten gave her a box of exploding paper balls, and Mary Lou Isleib a dribbling water glass. Selznick's present was a silver bracelet with a dangling heart, and the crew chipped in for roses. The total cost was $46.11.

Shirley's schedule was arranged so that she could fulfill both school and studio commitments. Westlake teachers prepared her assignments, which were completed between takes on the movie set and were returned to the school each week for grading.

Her social life was full, too. She gave parties in the elaborate Tudor-style playhouse on the grounds of the Temple four-acre estate. The huge main room now had a stage at one end with a movie screen which would retract at the touch of a button, and a duck pinball alley.

Shirley was now allowed to go on dates unchaperoned and had the normal teenager's interest in boys, especially those in uniform. In sprawling Los Angeles, gas rationing was a major factor of social life and young people checked their tanks before setting out. "Very often," says Shirley, "we'd turn off the motor and coast down hills and start it up again at the bottom."

She no longer rode horseback. When two of her friends were killed in accidents, Gertrude and the studio conferred and it was decided to sell her ponies.

When the Japanese attacked Pearl Harbor, Shirley's brother George, who had enlisted in the Marines, was stationed there. Two agonizing weeks passed before the Temples learned that he was safe. Then her other brother, Jack, enlisted in the corps, and Shirley threw herself headlong into all kinds of activity at home for the war effort.

She danced for hours with servicemen at the Hollywood Canteen. Like Bing Crosby, Bob Hope, Al Jolson, Betty Hutton and other Hollywood personalities, she toured shipyards, war plants and army posts entertaining, selling war bonds and trying to build morale. In one California shipyard, a little nervous because she was unused to playing before live audiences, she sang and danced for twenty thousand workers.

She visited hospitals and USO clubs and made radio broadcasts which were aired to servicemen all over the world. Her picture shared space on barracks walls with those of sexpots like Betty Grable and Lana Turner, and one Marine squadron adopted her as their "kid sister." At Westlake she joined in the precision drills of the school's "military corps," becoming one of its tiniest captains.

On one of her hospital visits, Shirley stopped at the bedside of a young soldier who was staring vacantly at the ceiling. "Is there anything I can do for you?" she asked.

The boy looked at her. "You're Shirley Temple," he said.

"Yes, is there anything you want?" Shirley asked.

"My leg's coming off tomorrow," he replied. "Would you stay with me while they do it?"

She would if the hospital authorities gave permission. The following morning, after obtaining the necessary consent, Shirley donned a white hospital uniform and kept her promise. When her Westlake classmates asked, "Shirley, how could you do it?" the reply came quietly and emphatically: "If he could stand having it off, I could stand helping him."

One afternoon, on a shopping expedition with some schoolmates in Beverly Hills, Shirley spotted Van Johnson (whom she had once described as part of a composite of her ideal man, the other half being the erudite sports columnist John Kieran) in a store. She waited outside until he emerged.

"He was looking down, so I shoved a piece of paper in his hand and asked him to please say 'Love to Shirley.'" Johnson began to autograph the paper without looking up until he heard her laugh.

"He did a perfect double take," Shirley says. "'Why, Temple,' he said, 'you little witch, you!'"

Secretary of the Treasury Morgenthau asked Shirley to help launch the sixth war loan drive in New York. Her parents accompanied her on the trip, which became a personal triumph for Shirley. At the St. Regis Hotel, where the Temples stayed, fans gathered early in the morning to get her autograph, which they

116

told her was worth two of Frank Sinatra. She met the mayor of New York, Fiorello La Guardia, went window-shopping, fed the pigeons in Central Park and saw the musical *Oklahoma!* On her last night, she went to the famous Stork Club, where owner Sherman Billingsley sent orchids and perfume to her table. As in earlier days, she attracted crowds wherever she went.

Her popularity delighted Selznick, who wrote in another memo:

> Shirley is exceedingly hot at the moment. We can't commence to fill demands for interviews and other press material on her from newspapers and magazines; and this is, of course, an indication of the interest of the public. At the previews of *I'll Be Seeing You*, co-starring Ginger Rogers, Joseph Cotten and Shirley Temple, Shirley's name was received with the biggest applause of all three despite the fact that the Gallup poll shows that Cotten is the new romantic rage, and that Ginger is one of the top stars in the business.
>
> Shirley's publicity in the New York press, both in connection with this appearance and in connection with her prior trip East to sell bonds, received more publicity—including, astonishingly, big front page breaks in the middle of a war—than I think has been accorded the visit of any motion picture star in New York in many, many years. Indeed it has been said . . . that her recent visit received more space than that of General de Gaulle. She has made a great hit in *Since You Went Away*; and her first grown-up part, that in *I'll Be Seeing You*, is a sensational success. Her fan mail is greater than that of any other star on our list—actually exceeding by a wide margin that of Ingrid Bergman, Jennifer Jones and Joan Fontaine, who are the next three, in that order.

As a senior at Westlake, Shirley wore the silver ring, given to seniors, inscribed with the school motto, *Possunt qui a posse Videntur* (They can because they think they can), at a dinner in the great hall at the beginning of the school year. She was a winsome, svelte and poised young woman with dark curly hair; the only trace of the old Shirley was found in the twinkling eyes and dimples. She dated often, her picture and name appearing in the columns with Nacio Herb Brown, a Hollywood song composer, co-star Guy Madison, Andy Hotchkiss, an old friend, and Maurice Prince, an army private.

Serious romance developed as she neared her seventeenth birthday. She had met handsome blond John Agar almost two years earlier when Ann Gallery, the daughter of ZaSu Pitts, brought him to a pool party at her home. Ann and her mother, the great comic character actress, were next-door neighbors.

The two stayed only a few minutes, but Shirley must have had some premonition of things to come because she told her mother he would be back. Some weeks later they met again at a tea given by ZaSu. John and his mother, Mrs. Lillian Agar, who operated a Beverly Hills boutique, were also guests.

"How about a double date this evening?" Ann suggested. Shirley agreed, but she went with a young Marine named Bud. John was Ann's date. There were a few more double dates, and then one night John called Shirley.

"How about going out by ourselves?" he suggested. Shirley agreed and he took her to a movie.

Agar, six foot three and as good-looking as any of her leading men, was a native of Lake Forest, Illinois, the grandson of a wealthy meat packer. His father, John George Agar, Sr., a former track and field star at the University of Chicago, died when his son was fourteen. John's mother opened a small, elegant store and acquired a wealthy clientele, and John was sent to the Pawling School in Dutchess County, New York. Later the family moved to Hollywood where Mrs. Agar opened another shop. In 1942 John went into the Army. When he met Shirley he was a sergeant stationed at the Fourth Air Force base in Ephrata, a remote town in the state of Washington. He was transferred to Oregon and Texas and finally to March Field, near Hollywood. He saw Shirley on weekends and when he was home on furlough.

John proposed to Shirley while his car was stopped for a traffic light on Sunset Boulevard, between a home for the aged and a gas station. Shirley remembers it was "the night the *Spellbound* music was played in the Hollywood Bowl." She accepted and they went

118

to tell the Temples. Gertrude urged them to keep the engagement secret at least until "after graduation." Although she herself had been a bride at seventeen, she had hoped Shirley would not follow her example.

But John gave Shirley a two-and-a-half-carat diamond engagement ring two weeks before her birthday, and she wasn't about to keep it in a drawer. She wore the ring under a glove to a luncheon for Westlake seniors in a Beverly Hills restaurant. She had to remove the glove to eat, the diamond flashed and the secret was out. The forty-two other members of the senior class began to squeal for details. Shirley later admitted she wanted them to be the first to know.

The Temples made it official that afternoon with an announcement issued by the Selznick International Studio. "It had not been planned to announce Shirley's engagement at this time, since both Shirley and John have promised that they do not intend to get married for two years, possibly three, and in any case Jack is in the army and his first duty is to his country," they said.

The engagement again put Shirley on the front pages. In Washington, Representative Gordon L. McDonough, a California Republican, told fellow members of the House that Shirley's engagement was "democracy in action." His voice trembling with emotion, McDonough declared, "We may rest assured that democracy is vigorously alive after reading the announcement recently made by Shirley Temple that she is engaged to an ordinary American soldier, GI John G. Agar, of Beverly Hills, California." Warming to his subject, he added, "Next to Roosevelt, Churchill and Stalin, Shirley Temple is one of the best-known individuals in the world, and unlike the Big Three she is the most beloved, with no opposition or enemies. All members of the House wish her long and blessed happiness."

Shirley received many letters from sixteen-year-olds asking her aid in countering parental objections to wartime romances. She replied that while it was all right to get engaged at seventeen, marriage should be postponed until a girl is nineteen or twenty.

In June, she was graduated from Westlake in outdoor ceremonies attended by her family and her boss, David O. Selznick.

With the other graduates, she wore a long, full-skirted gown of white tulle with a sweetheart neckline, lace bodice and three-quarter sleeves. Each of the girls carried a bouquet of pink roses.

Shortly after graduation, Shirley decided not to take her own advice. Fearing that John might still be sent overseas (the war would actually end in August 1945), she pushed up the date of the wedding to September 19, 1945. She was a few months past her seventeenth birthday.

10
"Baby" Takes a Vow

"We were young kids getting married. We were in love," says John Agar.

For almost thirty-five years, Agar has refused all interviews about his marriage to Shirley. He is speaking now for the first time of the events that created the turmoil in both their lives.

"I was still in the Army," he declares, "a staff sergeant, and I was given a ten-day furlough. We spent our honeymoon in Santa Barbara. Nobody knew where we were, though it seemed the entire world was trying to find out. It was a lovely, beautiful thing. All I can recall about the wedding was that there were people, an awful lot of people, outside the church on Wilshire Boulevard, and a lot of them inside."

It is understandable that his own wedding that Wednesday in September 1945 was a blur to John Agar.

He was unused to any of the eye-dazzling and mind-fuzzing glitter that greeted him as he arrived at the Wilshire Methodist Church. The scene resembled a Hollywood-style premiere. Crowds had begun gathering as early as three in the afternoon, and by eight that evening more than five thousand people lined the street, hopelessly snarling traffic on Wilshire Boulevard. Surging behind sawhorses and ropes, the throng was barely contained by some four dozen city, studio and military policemen. Once, the crowd crashed through the barricaded area in front of the church, sending a makeshift stand erected for photographers crashing into the street.

"I want an old-fashioned wedding," Shirley had said. "I don't want a Hollywood circus." It was a compromise: the public, eager to glimpse their child idol as a bride, got the circus outside, while inside the ceremony was a mix, part old-fashioned with a few unmistakable Hollywood touches.

The church was filled with flowers, hundreds of pink roses and more hundreds of pink-dyed daisies. The altar was banked high with blooms, and a broad blue ribbon was stretched down the long center aisle. Seven hundred invited guests were in their seats, listening to the melody of Irving Berlin's "Always." At 8:45, the song ended and, after several mellow chimes, a musical bridge to the triumphant *Lohengrin* wedding march, Shirley made her entrance on the arm of her father.

The timing was perfect. The guests had waited fifteen minutes longer than the scheduled hour for the wedding and were at the peak of expectancy but still short of impatience. The delay, however, was not Shirley's idea. Two of the most important guests, David Selznick and Governor Earl Warren of California, were late. They arrived breathless during "Always," slipped into their seats, and the wedding was on.

There were gasps as Shirley walked down the aisle. She looked like a princess come to life from a fairy tale, with her crown of corded looped satin, from which hung a long train, and her old-fashioned bodice-hugging short-sleeved dress of satin embroidered with seed pearls. She wore white wrist-length satin gloves with seed pearls and carried an orchid bouquet. And in her shoe was a penny for good luck.

John's sister Joyce, wearing a gown of "Shirley blue," was a bridesmaid, along with Mary Lou Isleib and five other young women. Shirley's matron of honor was Mrs. Jack Temple, and Jack was best man. George Junior and Sergeant Frank Walters, an army buddy, were among the seven ushers. Gertrude, dark and strikingly attractive, wore a dove-gray crepe dress and a tulle frilled hat, with long suede bead-studded gloves. In her hand was a spray of white orchids.

When Shirley reached the altar where John was waiting in his sergeant's uniform the lights dimmed and the area where they stood in front of Dr. Willsie Martin, pastor of the church, was bathed in soft candlelight. It was a nice, movie-like touch. Shirley and John, kneeling, took their vows, exchanged rings, and were pronounced man and wife. John then bestowed upon his bride a kiss which movie people among the guests said lasted longer than the censors would permit.

When they tried to leave by the front door, the circus took over again. The crowd crashed through the police lines, shouting, waving pencils and pads for autographs, reaching to touch them. John took one look at the sea of people lunging toward them and swung his bride back inside, shutting the door. A half hour later, a limousine drew up at a side door and they slipped out, heading for a reception at Shirley's estate.

Arriving guests walked across the grounds to the strains of Spanish guitars played by musicians in the courtyard, passed rose-filled gardens illuminated by multicolored lights, and entered a huge tent. A magnificent buffet supper awaited them on tables canopied by leaves entwined with roses.

Afterward, the guests were invited to the playhouse to view the wedding presents. There were enough gifts, covering nine tables, to stock a large, and expensive, specialty shop. One table glinted with hundreds of pieces of antique and modern sterling silver. Another was loaded with crystal goblets, dishes and serving pieces; one set alone came with eighteen of everything. On a third table were odds and ends—an 1820 English dish, a china serving set trimmed with twenty-two-carat gold, a tiny glass piano that opened to hold cigarettes—each lovely, each extremely costly. There were piles of towels and blankets, a number of fancy alarm clocks, electric irons, and four cookbooks.

At midnight, Shirley cut the wedding cake, which was almost as tall as she was, tossed her bouquet, and changed into her going-away clothes to drive across town with her new husband to the Los

Angeles Town House. At the desk, they discovered that the honeymoon suite they had reserved had been assigned mistakenly to an army officer and his bride, who had already retired. With profuse apologies, the Agars were given another suite, and Shirley remarked, "Well, at least I got my own husband."

After their idyllic week in Santa Barbara, she was back home and John was in Utah, expecting to be sent overseas. The orders never came. Earlier, in the spring of 1945, with German resistance collapsing in Europe, the Army had lowered the number of points required for discharge, and Agar, who could qualify, was mustered out.

When John came home, they talked over plans for their future. Home would be Shirley's "playhouse" on the Temple estate. John agreed, and Gertrude told her daughter she had better erect a fence between the big and little houses because she didn't want Shirley's dogs and children to be wandering on her property. Mother and daughter laughed, and plans went forward for the conversion of the play retreat into a newlywed home. While the plumbers and carpenters were at work, the Agars rented a little bungalow on San Vincente Boulevard in Santa Monica.

Almost every day, Shirley was there to watch the progress. When it was finished, it was the most magnificent dollhouse ever constructed for the habitation of people.

It had, to begin with, one of the Hollywood colony's largest and most luxurious living rooms, a two-story affair divided by clever furniture groupings into den, music room, dining and breakfast room. A butler's pantry led into a large kitchen at one end; at another was the bedroom, big enough to double as a study, and the bath. The stage, the movie screen and the projection booth were gone; the soda fountain was moved to the basement and equipped to dispense liquids with a more powerful jolt than syrup and soda water; and the dolls too were moved downstairs.

The decision to begin a new stage in her life, a phase calling for the exercise of a new maturity, in surroundings that bore such strong reminders of her childhood may have had a more significant impact on what followed than either expected. Nor can one discount the fact that the "playhouse" was only a short walk from Shirley's mother, who had molded her career and to whom she was so closely attached.

In these opulent surroundings, Shirley tried domesticity. She planned menus, went shopping and cooked—simple things such as steaks, lamb chops and chicken. When John said he preferred more elaborate fare, she made a stab at cuisine a little more *haute,* and even enrolled at a cooking school. Twice weekly she would don her old Westlake uniform, scrub her face of makeup, put up her hair and drive down to the Hillcliff Cooking School on Wilshire Boulevard for lessons. She would study there, unrecognized by the others, who were for the most part help sent by employees to hone their kitchen skills.

Toward the end of the five-week course, still incognito, Shirley enlivened a session by some play-acting. She averred that she too worked in a kitchen but for a dreadful employer, and proceeded to catalogue as many imaginary abuses as she could recall from her earlier movies. It was a good performance, so good that at the next class one of her audience took her aside and told her triumphantly that she had gotten her a new job with much nicer bosses. With Thursdays and Sundays off. Shirley thanked her and stammered that the boss seemed a little nicer and she'd stick it out for a while.

She went determinedly about her job as happy little homemaker. She kept the house neat, clean and even scrubbed, and she cooked a lot. This phase lasted about two months. Then she hired a housekeeper.

Her newest movie, *The Bachelor and the Bobby Soxer,* was keeping her too busy and too tired for domestic chores. The picture, with Cary Grant and Rudy Vallee, was a light summer show and a surprising hit that gave her career an upward lift.

Shirley, just over five feet and one hundred pounds, with a pert pretty face and a shapely figure, was no longer the adorable child but gave promise of becoming the adorable young girl.

Meanwhile, John too had become an actor. Selznick, appraising him at the wedding, had been impressed with his six-foot-two muscular body, his square chin, bright blue eyes, wavy brown hair and bashful grin. Figuring he could be developed into a major film star, Selznick called Agar and said, "Come on down and take a test. If you show any ability, and I think you will, I'll put you under contract."

Agar went to RKO-Radio, took the test, passed and was offered $150 a week. "Well," he recalls, "I had been making eighty-three dollars a month as a buck sergeant. It seemed like taking money under false pretenses, but he wanted me and I accepted. Besides, I felt it was something Shirley and I could do together."

Selznick, shrewdly capitalizing on the public's still-starry-eyed view of the couple, teamed them in *Fort Apache*, which was directed by John Ford and had a strong cast that included Henry Fonda, Victor McLaglen, Guy Kibbee and Irene Rich. Later, Shirley and John were paired again in *Adventure in Baltimore*, with Robert Young. The films made money, mostly because of the couple's box-office appeal, but Agar's movie career dimmed not long after the second was released in 1949.

Warner Brothers, believing that Shirley's name was still bankable, borrowed her for *That Hagen Girl*. She remembers it as "my favorite adult picture," but the critics were not enthralled. Bosley Crowther, calling the film "a bleak indiscretion," wrote that "poor little put-upon Shirley . . . looks most ridiculous through it all."

Before the film was finished, Shirley began experiencing the signs and symptoms of pregnancy. Visiting her doctor for tests, she asked him to telephone her on the set, give an assumed name and deliver a cryptic message that only the two of them would understand.

When the results were in, the doctor called and told her, "Mrs. Agar, this is the florist. Your roses will be delivered sometime next winter. I think it will be a very fine selection." She told only Mary Lou Isleib, who whooped with glee. Then she rushed home when filming was finished and broke the news to John. "Then we went over to Mother's," Shirley recalls. "All she did was look at my face and sat down, smiling and crying all at once."

Selznick, counting heavily on the resurgence of his star at the box office, reacted differently. When Shirley bounced into his office and announced her pregnancy, he said nothing, sat down hard and clasped his head in his hands. With him was Daniel O'Shea, his executive vice-president and later president of RKO. O'Shea, equally silent, walked to the window and stared out.

Shirley commented on their woeful response the following year, when she turned twenty-one, in an article in *Modern Screen*, a leading fan magazine. "You'd have thought I was going to commit suicide or something," she wrote.

It was a flip remark, yet a curious one.

Only a few months afterward, she almost did just that.

Shirley, age one. The curls were just beginning to form. *UPI*

Shirley autographed her picture "To President Roosevelt, love, Shirley Temple." *Courtesy Franklin D. Roosevelt Library*

Shirley (center) and fellow members of the Baby Burlesks don street clothes for an ice cream and cake party.

Jack Hays, producer of the Baby Burlesks series, gives Shirley pointers for her portrayal of Morelegs Sweettrick in *Kids 'n' Hollywood*.

She won first prize in the bathing beauty contest but Shirley still had to scrub floors to earn her keep in *Kids 'n' Hollywood*.

In *Glad Rags to Riches,* Shirley was a nightclub entertainer and sang her first song in a movie.

Shirley, with the help of her mother, autographed her picture for Jay Gorney who "started me in pictures on the Fox lot." *Courtesy Sandra Gorney*

She was a sturdy little girl and loved to play. This bike, which she used when the family vacationed at Palm Springs, was a favorite. *Courtesy Museum of Modern Art/Film Stills Archive*

After Shirley's success in *Stand Up and Cheer*, Gertrude Temple negotiated a new contract and signs the documents to the approval of Shirley and George Temple. *UPI*

Studio publicists manufactured a feud between Shirley and
Jane Withers who played her sharp-tongued foil in *Bright Eyes*.

On loan to Paramount, Shirley charms Warren Hymer and
Adolphe Menjou (right) in *Little Miss Marker*.

Shirley and George Murphy, later the Republican Senator from California, in *Little Miss Broadway*.

Bill Robinson taught Shirley several of her tap routines, including this one in *Rebecca of Sunnybrook Farm*.

Shirley and Arthur Treacher
appeared together in several movies.
They are shown here in *Heidi*.

A sailor-suited Shirley grins
on the set of *Captain January*.

Victor McLaglen and Shirley aim their guns at
rebellious natives in *Wee Willie Winkie*.

In *The Littlest Rebel* Shirley, a Southern belle, goes to see President Abraham Lincoln to plead for the release of her father who had been captured by Union Troops.

Eleanor Roosevelt visits with Shirley and her parents on the set in Hollywood. *Courtesy Franklin D. Roosevelt Library*

Claudette Colbert won the best actress award in 1934 for *It Happened One Night* and Shirley got a special miniature Oscar. *Academy of Motion Picture Arts and Sciences*

Shirley Temple presents an Oscar and seven little Oscars to Walt Disney at the 1938 awards dinner of the Academy of Motion Picture Arts and Sciences. *Academy of Motion Picture Arts and Sciences*

Fox's top money-makers, Shirley and Will Rogers, were fast friends. *The Watson Family's Photographic Archives*

Film star Janet Gaynor and Shirley get together for a bit of gossip on the Fox set. *Courtesy Museum of Modern Art/Film Stills Archive*

Shirley and George Temple and the family pet share a bicycle at the Desert Inn at Palm Springs, California. *Courtesy Museum of Modern Art/Film Stills Archive*

Jay Gorney, Broadway and Hollywood composer, found Shirley in the lobby of a movie theater and pushed her for a role in Fox's *Stand Up and Cheer. Courtesy Sandra Gorney*

As she matured,
studio executives tried to
create a glamor girl image.

Annette Funicello accepts
honorary juvenile award from
Shirley for Hayley Mills, not
present, in 1960. *Academy of
Motion Picture Arts and Sciences*

Shirley and her most famous leading man—President Ronald Reagan—
in a scene from *That Hagen Girl*, 1947.

Mr. and Mrs. John Agar on the steps of the Wilshire Methodist Church after their marriage in 1945. *Courtesy Museum of Modern Art/Film Stills Archive*

Shirley and first husband, John Agar, show off their new daughter, Linda Susan, to the press.

Shirley and second husband, Charles Black, in their first appearance before the press a few days after their secret 1950 wedding in his family's home. *UPI*

Mrs. Black, a suburban matron, reads to her children, Lori, Linda Susan and Charles, Jr., in their Atherton home.

Appointed by President Nixon to the American delegation to the 24th General Assembly of the United Nations, Shirley Temple Black leaves the U.S. mission offices in September 1969. *UPI*

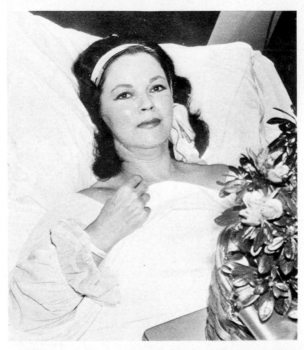

Shirley, in her hospital bed at the Stanford Medical Center, shortly after she underwent surgery for removal of a breast in 1972. *UPI*

Chief of Protocol Black introduces Urho Kekkonen, president of Finland, to President Ford and Mrs. Betty Ford during 1976 ceremonies on the White House Lawn. *UPI*

11

Paradise Lost

Despite glowing, and cloying, stories in the newspapers and magazines of their blissful life together, there was trouble in the playhouse.

Linda Susan, seven pounds, six ounces, was born shortly after dawn on January 29, 1948, in Santa Monica Hospital, where Shirley herself had come into the world twenty-one years before. "SHIRLEY HAS REAL LIFE DOLLY OF HER OWN," the *New York Daily News* announced.

But the marriage had begun to fade much earlier, and on December 5, 1949, Shirley went into a Los Angeles courtroom to ask for a divorce. She told a shocking story of a marriage gone very wrong.

Rumors had surfaced soon after the glittering wedding that all was not well. Despite denials by each of them, it became increasingly clear to intimates of the couple that the fairy-tale romance was cracking apart. Shirley, of course, knew it, too, and was confused and intensely unhappy. By the fall of 1949, there was no longer any hope of their remaining together.

In October she cried for two weeks without letup before she finally decided to end the marriage. On October 13 she told Virginia MacPherson of the United Press, "I don't know whether it's

Jack's fault or mine. All I know is there's no chance of a reconcilia-
tion. . . . We've both tried very hard. But it wouldn't work."

She said she would like to keep the divorce "as dignified and
quiet as possible." An action was filed by her attorney, George
Stahlman, citing "mental cruelty," standard for Hollywood divorce
suits.

On Friday, December 3, she sat down in her bedroom to answer
a fan letter from a young woman who had written to her many
times before. In her latest note, Marian Kruse of Villa Park, Illinois,
had said she had just became engaged. Shirley intended to write a
brief note of congratulations but ended up pouring out the feelings
she had bottled up for so long.

"I was fully conscious of the reaction my filing for divorce would
arouse," Shirley wrote to Marian, who is now Mrs. Joseph Alessi.
The letter, in a frame, hangs on her bedroom wall:

> My decision was heartbreaking to me and was not made
> until I had prayed and hoped that things would be otherwise.
> In the hours, days and weeks I spent hoping this action never
> would have to be taken, I thought first of my baby. She
> means all to me. Then I thought of those who loved me and
> would feel I was disappointing them in seeking divorce.
>
> For two years I have made every effort to save my mar-
> riage, so you can know I have not been hasty. The trivial
> matters you have read about in the press certainly could not
> cause my decision. The reasons go deep and hurtful in my
> heart and that is why, knowing full well that I would be
> judged in many degrees, I concluded that I just could not go
> on any longer. I ask only that judgment of my decision be not
> based upon these reports.
>
> I want you to know that neither career, fame nor anything
> in this world means more to me than love and respect. Please
> don't let rumors, innuendos or cruel gossip influence you. I
> just want to assure you that I would not have taken this step
> without having taken every means to avoid it.
>
> As for Linda Susan, I have the most precious baby in the
> world and it was she of whom I thought every one of the sad

moments I spent before deciding I had to do what I have done.

I have written much more than I intended when I started this letter, but you took a lot of time in writing me and I give you as much in return. May I extend you my kindest regards and understand that I shall be grateful for your prayers and your considered judgment.

At 9 A.M. the following Monday, Shirley arrived at Superior Court accompanied by two attorneys, her father and a corroborating witness, Alice Franklin, who had been a Westlake classmate. Fifteen minutes later Judge Roy Herndon mounted the bench, and Shirley, wearing a simple tailored gray wool suit and a navy-blue hat with matching gloves, walked to the witness stand.

A packed courtroom heard Shirley, until then worshiped, imitated, universally loved and, above all, emotionally unscarred, tell the melancholy story of her first real adversity.

"Difficulties" had arisen only five months after the ceremony, she said, and involved her husband's failure to come home on time, neglect of her when they were together in public, and a fondness for liquor and other women.

At one point in her fifteen-minute appearance, she stunned the spectators with the disclosure that her multiplying problems had been so overwhelming that they led to a momentary thought of suicide. Once in the middle of the night, after an especially wrenching experience, she had become "very upset." Blinded by tears, she had rushed outside. "I jumped into my car and was going to drive over a cliff," she testified. But she had regained her emotional balance and, instead of heading toward the canyons, she drove to the home of her doctor and woke him. When she calmed down she returned home, but the doctor, concerned about her after she had told him of her state of mind, insisted on following her in his car.

The testimony concluded, Judge Herndon noted that the court "cannot fail to take notice of the well-known fact that this plaintiff occupies a special place in the hearts and affections of millions of people, not only in the state but throughout the country." The court, he said, was committed to the established policy of California "that no divorce shall be granted except upon grounds which our law recognizes as sufficient. Fairness to the plaintiff, however, required this court to declare that the evidence which has been offered here, the plaintiff's demeanor and the very evident sincerity with which she testified have convinced the court the grounds . . . are serious and substantial. . . ."

At 9:47, just thirty-two minutes after Shirley took the stand, Judge Herndon granted an interlocutory decree which would become final after a year, gave her custody of Linda Susan and restored her maiden name. He ordered Agar to pay $100 a month for the support of his twenty-two-month-old daughter. Shirley, a millionaire, had not asked for alimony, nor was there any community property to be shared.

Agar, who did not contest the divorce, was making a stage appearance three thousand miles away in Buffalo, New York, when the decree was granted. He had said little to reporters, who had hounded him ever since Shirley announced their separation. His lawyer, Clore Warne, told the judge that Agar had "conducted himself as a gentleman throughout all the conferences for settlement" and was concerned only with the welfare of his wife and daughter. Now, besieged by newspersons at his hotel, he seemed on the verge of tears. About Shirley's testimony he would only say, "it reflects inaccurately our real differences." Pressed for his version, he would say no more. "No constructive purpose would be served by recriminations or airing our respective sides in public," he told them.

The end of the marriage was a psychological blow to Americans whose notions of love, romance and human behavior had been shaped by the movies and the stars who played in them. There were already two generations of men and women who had spent hours in darkened theaters every week, and they wanted, indeed yearned, to believe what they were watching. It was only a short mental step to transfer that faith to the heroes and heroines acting out the stories. The tell-all era, with its confessional of the most explicit sexual encounters and flagrant infidelities, was still a quarter of a century away. Stars were *stars*, with feet shod in imported leather and silver slippers, not encased in clay. In an oral history on the performing arts on file at Columbia University, Albert Delacorte, son of the founder of the Dell Publishing Company, said, "They [the moviegoers] like to believe that marriage is forever, they like to believe there is such a thing as true love."

It hurt them to hear otherwise. The hurt was especially severe in the case of Shirley Temple. When Elsa Maxwell, the celebrity hostess and social arbiter, went on a national lecture tour, she found herself besieged. "They wrote me bags full of letters deploring the end of the marriage," she said. "Girls waited at the stage door of the theaters where I spoke, sometimes red-eyed. They all said the same thing: 'Tell us why Shirley did that. We can't bear it.'"

Shirley herself understood the reaction clearly. "When two people are put on a pedestal of perfection, painted perpetually in rosy tints with everything so beautiful," she said, "the disillusionment, when it comes, is a hundred times as great." Only a few weeks after the wedding, she and John were photographed for a magazine in many "lovey-dovey poses," a dream couple living a dream life. "You can't escape that 'perfect' buildup," she said, "but it makes the breakdown, if it comes, a great shock."

The public was grieving for her, and for itself. Those who had viewed her films and had seen that the bleakest and blackest situations were always resolved in the final reels lamented for her, and at the same time felt a threat to themselves. As long as things had come out all right for Shirley at "The End," there was a hope, subliminal perhaps, that troubles could be resolved, somehow and in some way, for everyone. When things, unexpectedly, turned out all wrong in Shirley's personal crisis, faith was shaken.

The public had rooted for the marriage because, in its innocence, it truly believed in the happy-ever-after myth nurtured by the movies. That Shirley too put her faith in its longevity is undeniable. It was only afterward, as she sat alone in her house on the grand estate with her now-toddling two-year-old daughter, that she realized it had been a terrible mistake. "It never should have happened," she said.

Looking back when she turned thirty, she said that if a girl wishes to marry at sixteen or seventeen, she should choose a part-ner she grew up with—"a childhood sweetheart, the boy next door or someone she has known all her life." Then, in an obvious per-sonal reference, she added, "At that young age a girl does not have enough judgment to trust herself when she's swept off her feet by a comparative stranger."

Shirley recognized at thirty that thirteen years earlier she had, along with many other girls of her generation, fallen victim to peer pressure. At Westlake, the senior girls competed for practically everything—for grades, a place on the hockey team, editorial posts on school publications, but most of all the glorious honor of being the first to sport an engagement ring, the first to marry and the first to have a baby.

"I wanted to win the race," Shirley admits, and adds, "This is a dangerous basis for marriage."

Observers who knew them both believe that Gertrude actually helped propel Shirley into the very marriage she hoped would not take place.

Sidney Skolsky: "She got married early to get away from her mother. She wanted to be on her own. Wanted to break away from the kind of life she was leading. Her mother and father considered her always as the child star, and she was growing up. This hap-pens often with child movie stars. They want to get away from their parents and strike out on their own.

"She wasn't oppressed at home, that's not what I mean. But she didn't like being told what to do by her mother, who was sitting on the set all the time, every picture, every minute, and criticizing, sometimes good, sometimes bad, what Shirley had done.

"She didn't resent her mother when she was younger. She en-joyed it while she was a kid. It was after she came of age that she had enough.

"The marriage failed because she wasn't ready for it. Later, when she developed as a person, she married and remained mar-ried. She had become a woman by then."

Dorothy Manners: "I wouldn't doubt that she got married to get away from her mother and her protected life and start having her own life. Marriage was an escape for her."

Rudy Vallee, who acted with her in *The Bachelor and the Bobby Soxer* in 1947, while she was still wed to Agar, was cynical even then. Vallee, college-educated and shrewd in the ways of show business, of just plain business and of love, says, "Agar was the type of person Shirley never should have married. She needed a stable businessman, with a lot of money and a college background. He was a handsome lad, a fine personable lad, but they were mismatched."

Gertrude tried hard not to "dominate" her daughter, Elsa Maxwell wrote, but it was a resolution not easy to keep. Said Maxwell, "Mrs. Temple, like any other mother, would be quick to see Shirley standing awkwardly, wearing an untidy blouse, needing her hair brushed. And since everything Shirley did was important, Mrs. Temple was quicker to speak than another mother might have been."

Only a half year before Shirley was to become a wife, Gertrude cautioned that she was smiling too broadly, driving too fast and letting her dress fall too low, said Maxwell. "No one ever doubted that Shirley resented this, devoted as she is to her mother."

A Talk With John Agar

The extraordinarily handsome John Agar turned sixty-two in 1982 and, in maturity, is an extraordinarily handsome older man, with a full head of white hair, bright-blue eyes and a strong chin.

He is still an actor; through the years he has appeared in some seventy movies and television series, though no longer in starring roles. He is proud of the fact that he played in many John Wayne pictures; the last one was *Big Jake* in 1971. But acting could not provide a steady income, so for a time he sold automobiles for a Los Angeles Mercedes-Benz dealer and later became an executive with an insurance firm. Now, between acting jobs, he is the senior citizens' promotion director in southern California for the Brunswick recreation centers.

He discussed his bittersweet recollections of his marriage to Shirley Temple and some of the reasons why it collapsed.

John Agar: "I look back on those years as though it all happened to a stranger. It's hard, close to impossible, for me even to recognize that young man. Everything about me—my attitudes toward life, my values, my faith in God—has changed so much since those long-ago days.

"Some things stand out clearer than others. One day in 1949 seems like yesterday. I came home in the afternoon and there was Shirley's attorney in the living room. I asked him where she was. He said she was in the bedroom.

"I wanted to know why he was there and what he wanted. He told me, 'Shirley wants a divorce.'

"I didn't believe it, and I told him so. I said I wanted to talk to Shirley, but he said she didn't want to see me. It hit me right between the eyes. I felt that while there had been problems in our marriage, there weren't any that couldn't be resolved.

"In a few minutes, I left without seeing Shirley and drove to my mother's house. I told her what was going to happen and I remember she cried.

"Then the roof caved in. The newspapers never stopped calling, day and night. Reporters did everything in the world to get me to talk, begging, arguing, even offering me large sums of money. I turned them all down. When we separated, Shirley and I made an agreement that we would not say anything negative about each other to the newspapers and magazines. I was raised to be a gentleman, and saying anything uncomplimentary about one's wife, which is what everyone was demanding of me, was certainly not gentlemanly. Wasn't then and isn't now.

"I had some pretty bad times after the divorce.

"I drank a lot more than I should and, very foolishly, got behind the wheel of an automobile. A judge called me a potential killer on the highway, and he was absolutely right. One memory that burns in my brain is being thrown into the Los Angeles County Jail for four months because I had violated my probation after a drunken-driving conviction. There were seventy-five other prisoners—rapists, arsonists, and gunmen—in a cellblock built to house thirty-six. I slept on a mattress placed on a stone floor.

"Those were dark days, the worst of my life. Two things kept me

136

going then. Without them, I'm damn sure I would have slipped lower and lower, and eventually been destroyed. One was my wife, Loretta. Loretta has been at my side ever since we were married in 1951. My second source of strength was, and still is, God.

"Well, thirty years have gone by since then, and those bulwarks of strength are with me still. Loretta and I have two wonderful adopted sons, Martin David, twenty-five, and John George, eighteen. I can say with a full heart that I am a happy man.

"That marriage long ago is now part of motion picture history, I suppose. It failed, I feel, because we were just too young. Shirley was only seventeen, and I was twenty-four. Oh, sure, kids that age can get over the roadblocks of early marriage, though it's not easy, but our situation had its own very unique problems.

"Shirley Temple was a legend, a world-famous movie star, and I was a kid from Chicago who had been tossed into a lifestyle unlike any I had ever known. I was a stranger in a strange land. I grew up in Lake Forest, which was a pretty suburb with large, comfortable homes, and mine was one of them. But that didn't last very long. In 1935, when I was fourteen, my dad died and I became the man of the family. . . .

"It was very foreign to me to be married to a famous person. I had never experienced anything like it before. Putting it simply, I was beyond my depth.

"And you've got to remember that Shirley was even more than a movie star. She was a national institution. I didn't have the background, nor the experience, nor the maturity, to handle my marriage to her.

"I liked Shirley's parents. They were good, decent people and there was never any in-law trouble. Mrs. Temple was always very nice to me, and as for her father, George, he was one heck of guy. He loved to play golf and we went out together many times. We'd call each other when there was a good wrestling match in the area, and we'd go.

"We had it all, Shirley and I, for a while—the beautiful home, complete with tropical fish, dogs and parakeets, a swimming pool, even an outdoor refrigerator. We had everything any young couple could want, except what was needed to make it all work into a real marriage.

"I returned to Hollywood from my stage tour two weeks after the divorce. The following week, I went to the Brentwood house with two imported French dolls for Susan. After that, I saw my daughter every week or two until she was six.

"I talked to Linda Susan the night of her sixth birthday—on January 29, 1954, it was. Then Shirley, who had remarried, moved to Washington with her husband and Linda. That was the last time I saw or spoke to my daughter.

"I know that I was made the heavy in the case. The press, as well as the motion picture industry, aimed a lot of potshots at me. I took the strongest barrage they had and I survived. The press predicted that my marriage to Loretta would last less than six months. We proved them wrong.

"I've made mistakes, but show me the man who has not. I read about Shirley in the newspapers and she has a happy, fulfilled life. I'm glad about that. I wish her nothing but the best.

"I am at peace with myself. The past is past and I do not look over my shoulder often, if at all."

12

"Some Enchanted Evening"

Shirley's reaction to the curiosity, the gossip and the glaring head-lines which followed her courtroom testimony was predictable. She became a very private person, desperately trying to avoid the constant scrutiny to which she had been subjected for many years. With Susan, now a rambunctious two-year-old, she went back to the playhouse, refusing even to consider living with her parents in their big house nearby.

"I'm an adult," she declared. "I'm the mother of a child and I'm quite independent. It's nice to be able to run over and see them when I please. But this is my house and this is where Susan and I belong."

She spent hours with her, pushing the child's bedtime back several hours so they could have dinner together. Afterward the two would curl up in a big armchair, a newly acquired Great Dane puppy huddled at their feet, and listen to old Temple records. Shirley had three that featured medleys of her songs, and Susan insisted that "On the Good Ship *Lollipop*," "An Old Straw Hat" and "Dreamland Choochoo" be played each night before she would consent to being put to bed.

Occasionally Shirley would visit old friends, but after a few nights out brought more newspaper speculation, she was rarely seen in public. She refused any further comment on her marriage and divorce, contending it was all behind her.

"It's senseless, like talking about an operation," she declared. "The sooner you stop, the sooner you start feeling better."

After Susan was asleep, Shirley thought a lot about her future. Her contract with David Selznick ran for several more months; she had a picture scheduled with Warner Brothers, but she was not happy with the roles she had been getting. She told friends she might write a book about her Hollywood experiences. Or study languages. Or learn to paint. She had always been interested in surgery; maybe she would become a nurse or work in a hospital.

It was obvious to those who knew her that she was casting about for something to channel her energies. When Selznick suggested she go to Europe to study acting, perhaps even change her name to insure anonymity, she refused.

"For the first and only time in my life, I didn't like men at all," she declared.

Why did Shirley fade from films? Here are explanations from those who knew and worked with her:

Allan Dwan: "She outgrew her charm."

Sidney Skolsky: "She outgrew her talent."

Dorothy Manners: "She never developed sex appeal. She was not Elizabeth Taylor, who, even as a child, had an obvious and powerful sexual attraction and, of course, more and more of it as she grew older."

Rudy Vallee: "She was attractive as a young woman but not beautiful enough. Moviegoers could not admire her as a gorgeous creature. Furthermore, she was hard to fit into roles because she was tiny and only fairly attractive. Besides, I don't think she cared all that much either. She had enough money to take it easy. I think she just didn't give a damn whether she made it or not."

Henry Hathaway: "She didn't want to be second-rate."

If Shirley had come along in her teens without the momentum of her earlier career, it is doubtful if anyone would have paid any attention to her at all. Professor William K. Everson, the film historian, says, "She belonged exactly where she began, as a child star in the innocent 1930s. After that, the special appeal she had as a child didn't work anymore. She became just another pretty little actress in the movies. There were so many others like her, some as good, some better, some as pretty, some prettier. She was no longer unique. The same applied in a different degree to Jackie Coogan, who was an incredibly appealing child but the older he got the more routine and ordinary he became, and the talent wasn't able to sustain a continuing acting career."

One January afternoon, George Temple stopped by the play-house with a suggestion that, unbeknownst to them, would chart Shirley's future.

"Susu's going to have a birthday next week," he pointed out. "Let's celebrate. My treat and Mother's. Pick a number from one to three. Palm Springs. Phoenix. Hawaii." Shirley had been to Hawaii three times as a child—in 1935, 1937 and 1939—and she remembered the friendliness of the people, the miles of beautiful beaches and the bright-blue water of the ocean. It had been a happy, magical time, and, hoping to recapture those feelings, she chose the island again.

When they could not get shipboard reservations, Shirley, by now eagerly looking forward to a change of scene, persuaded the Temples to fly. "Look, we'll all be together," she told her reluctant parents. "If anything happens, it'll happen to all of us."

Visitors arriving at Hawaii by boat are traditionally welcomed at the dock by lei-carrying islanders who drape their shoulders with flowers. Those coming by plane usually miss this. Surprisingly, the day Shirley was expected groups of people began arriving at the airport at 5:30 A.M. When the clipper plane finally landed at 9:15, there were about three thousand adults and children, carrying leis and cameras, assembled at the airfield. Welcoming cheers broke out as Shirley disembarked. "I felt," she said later, "as if I'd come home."

Shirley swam, soaked up the sun and played on the beach with Susan. She took her to see how pineapples and sugarcane grew. Old friends called and brought their children to play with Susan. For the first time in months Shirley began to relax; so the Temples moved from a hotel to a house on the beach at Kalianiole Road near Diamond Head, and the two-week vacation was extended to six.

One night Shirley was invited to a luau, a Hawaiian feast where the main dish, roast pig, is cooked in underground ovens. Susan selected the dress she wanted her mother to wear, a frilly white gown with a décolletage of white flowers, and watched as Shirley brushed her curls and tied them with a black velvet bow. Soon after she arrived at the party, she met a tall, darkly handsome man, an American working in Honolulu, probably one of the few persons who had never seen a Temple movie. His name was Charles Alden Black.

Actually they might have met a few days earlier if Black had not been such an avid surfer. "I was supposed to go to a reception for her when a friend called to say the surf was up," Black explains. "I just forgot about Shirley Temple and went surfing."

Before the evening was over, he asked her to dinner and Shirley accepted. For the rest of the vacation, they dated constantly.

"I really wasn't very interested in meeting Shirley Temple," Black explains. "I was living a very full life of my own and—well, I just didn't care."

"It's corny, but it's all true," Shirley says. "You know, some enchanted evening across a crowded room. We haven't had an uncrowded moment since."

Black, thirty, came from a socially prominent San Francisco family. His father, James Byers Black, was president of the Pacific Gas and Electric Company, the largest public utility in California. He was a self-made man who had started his very successful business career in 1912 as an inspector for the Great Western Power Company. He was a prominent clubman, a member of the advisory council of the School of Business of the University of California and an avid patron of music and ballet.

But Charles Black decided early on to make it on his own. By the time he was sixteen, an independent and adventurous spirit caused him to work his way, during school vacations, to Hong Kong and Tahiti. He went to the Hotchkiss Preparatory School, obtained his bachelor's degree at Stanford University and, in 1941, enlisted in the Navy.

142

He had a brilliant record in World War II but passes it off, saying simply, "I was in the Navy." One of his friends comments, "The truth of the matter is that he was in naval intelligence and he pulled off some of the most dangerous missions of the war." Black's naval career included service in the Solomon Islands, New Guinea, the Philippines, the Dutch East Indies and China. He was awarded the Silver Star and a Presidential Citation after a daring maneuver in which he landed from a submarine on Japanese-held islands to determine the enemies' troop strength.

His war service over, Black enrolled in the Harvard School of Business Administration. When he returned to San Francisco, instead of working for his father, he joined the Golden State Milk Company and peddled milk door to door, rising to assistant sales manager within a year. From that position, he moved to Hawaii as assistant to the president of the Hawaiian Pineapple Company.

Bright, athletic, attractive, Black had become a much-sought-after bachelor on the Hawaiian social scene. Then he met Shirley and was no longer available.

When the Temples ended their Hawaiian stay in the middle of March and went back to California, Black flew there to see Shirley. A few weeks later he resigned his position and left Honolulu for San Francisco. That weekend, Shirley was his date for the Bachelor's Ball, one of the highlights of San Francisco's social season. He took her to meet his parents, who were staying at the Cypress Point Club on the Monterey Peninsula. They went hiking, Shirley unrecognized in blue jeans, a bandanna around her hair, and to the Stanford–Army game, where they sat for hours in the rain.

Black went to work for television station KITV in Los Angeles, and rumors began to surface that they would marry. One afternoon they were driving and Shirley flicked on the radio. "Shirley Temple," she heard, "will soon announce her engagement to Charles Black, son of the president of Pacific Gas and Electric."

"We just about had a wreck," Shirley commented, denying the engagement. "We're just good friends." She repeated the denial on December 6 when her divorce decree became final. "I have no plans to get married during the holiday season," she said. "In fact, I have no plans to get married at all. I'm too busy getting ready for

Christmas. My daughter, Susie, is all excited about it. I'm going to take her downtown to see Santa Claus next week."

The statement may have been camouflage to throw the press off the trail as Shirley and Charles, once she was free, made a quick decision. The next day, Charles asked Superior Judge Henry Jorgensen of Salinas to perform the wedding ceremony, and on December 15 he and Shirley quietly drove to Salinas to get a marriage license.

They were married Saturday, December 16, at 4:30 P.M., in a simple ceremony in the living room of the white California-style ranch home of the groom's father in Monterey. The only guests were members of the two families. Plans had been closely guarded, and news of the marriage was not revealed until Shirley and Black had left to honeymoon at an undisclosed location. Black's mother confirmed the marriage but said she was under orders to reveal no details.

Judge Jorgensen, who performed the ceremony in front of a fireplace decorated with flowers and pine boughs, predicted that the "marriage should last forever."

"In my twenty-three years of marrying people," he declared, "I've never seen a happier couple."

On their return from their honeymoon, Shirley and Black, with Susan, lived in a house in Bel-Air and he worked for KITV until he was recalled to active duty with the Navy during the Korean conflict. A lieutenant commander in the naval reserve, he was assigned to duty at the Pentagon in Washington, and they had to move east.

Black rented a white house set on two acres on River Road, in the hunt country section of Bethesda, Maryland, so tiny, said movie columnist Hedda Hopper, that it could fit into the living room of Shirley's Brentwood home. It had a fourteen-by-fourteen-foot living room, a miniscule den, three bedrooms and two and a half baths. There were flowering dogwood trees in the back and a broad grassy lawn which Shirley often trimmed herself with a neighbor's tractor.

The lawn was overgrown with three-foot-high weeds when they

moved in. Shirley, unfamiliar with East Coast flowers, thought they were pretty and filled all the vases in the house. "Immediately Charlie and I started sneezing—and came down with hay fever. Too late I read a warning in the paper not to pick ragweed and not to bring it into the house."

Shirley's presence in the neighborhood attracted many tourists who did not recognize her. Once she was on the tractor when a man, driving by, called out angrily to her to get out of the way so he could take a picture of Shirley Temple's house.

Shirley shopped in the local supermarket a few miles down the road, did her own cooking and cleaning, and looked after Susan. She was washing up the breakfast dishes one morning when the doorbell rang. Wiping her hands on a towel, she opened the door to a half-dozen high-school students assigned to get a story on Shirley Temple for the school newspaper. "You couldn't," they gasped in disbelief, "be Shirley Temple?"

"I was quite disturbing to them," Shirley says, "a housewife and famous movie star doing her own housework."

The Blacks socialized with navy personnel (Shirley would get a mess boy from the officers' club to mix drinks and pass hors d'oeuvres) and were frequent guests at embassy parties. She recalls, "I loved Washington. It has such a small-town air about it. I was pregnant most of the time, or so it seemed. When I look at pictures of myself at embassy parties, I get bigger and bigger."

Charles Junior was born two weeks early in the Bethesda Naval Hospital. The baby, eight and a half pounds, was delivered by Caesarean section after Shirley went into labor and doctors discovered that the umbilical cord was wrapped around its neck. The Blacks had made arrangements for Shirley's delivery at the naval hospital at the suggestion of an old friend, Dan Kimball, who was undersecretary of the navy. "Since your husband is in the Navy," he asked, "why don't you make all the other young navy wives proud to have their babies in a naval hospital?"

Shirley was awake throughout the forty-five minute operation, which began at 1 A.M. She lay on the operating table watching the reflections of the doctors and nurses in the lamp overhead. As the surgery got under way, the doctor made a vertical incision down her abdomen. A short while later, Shirley, who had previously observed many operations, asked for a towel to shield her eyes.

"I had had my fill of my own operation," she said later.

Everything seemed fine. The next morning after she saw her baby, a nurse told her to walk to the doctor's office for an examination. Shirley didn't feel like walking, but the nurse said it was important for new mothers to walk as soon as possible.

Shirley followed orders and discovered several hours later that the activity caused her stitches to break open and that further surgery was needed. For six weeks she was desperately ill. She suffered four separate crises—a pulmonary embolism in her left lung, pneumonitis, pleurisy and peritonitis. She was moved from maternity to the intensive-care section of surgery. Her parents flew east, but only Black was allowed into her room.

One night, in great pain, she lay alone, pressing a soda bottle against her left side for relief. She worried that the clot might break loose and travel to her brain, with the gravest consequences. She stared at the whirring blades of the electric fan and began to see the faces of long-dead relatives and friends—her grandmother, Warner Baxter, Bill Robinson.

"Come on up, Shirley," the dancer seemed to be saying, "it's just wonderful up here. Come on up and we'll have a real good time." Shirley called for the nurse and begged not to be left alone.

Three critical days followed, during which her family and the hospital personnel feared for her life. Finally her condition began to improve, and several weeks after the baby's birth she was discharged from the hospital.

Black took his wife and son back to the Bethesda house, where Shirley, many weeks before, had carefully arranged Susan's bassinet and nursery paraphernalia for the new baby. A nurse looked after the infant while Shirley regained her strength.

Black's tour of duty was over in the spring of 1953 and he was discharged by the Navy. He and Shirley said goodbye to Washington friends, stopping at the White House to see President Eisenhower. They shipped their belongings west and began to drive cross-country with the two children.

Back in Hollywood after a leisurely trip, which included roadside picnics wherever possible, Shirley said her first priority was to find a suitable house. She had no immediate plans to return to acting. Charles, she said, would "look into the business end of television."

.

13

Profile at Thirty

She was prettier than she ever was, or would be. The fat pads of early adulthood were gone from her face, leaving a pink-and-white oval—shaped, some remarked, like a perfectly proportioned lozenge. The hazel eyes, which had been threatening to turn brown, finally had done so; and the hair, worn in a short cut with soft waves, had darkened by itself into the same rich hue. There was not a trace of gold or ringlets.

Her weight was 110, which she decided to trim down to 107 and succeeded. She was tiny even in high heels, not a millimeter taller than the five feet two (and a bit over) she had been as a junior miss. Her manner in public was distant, sometimes aloof; it was not the coldness it may have appeared to be, but shyness and the wariness that people lionized by the public often wrap around themselves. In private, when she became excited about things, which was often, the reserve vanished and her voice, a well-modulated alto, took on a contagious animation. Then the eyes, which she used with the artfulness of an accomplished actress, would dance.

When she smiled, the dimples appeared. They were the sole remaining link between the attractive, well-groomed, affluent young matron and the little moppet of the movies.

At thirty, the star was a figure from another world, someone she looked upon with a cool detachment. "I have little time to give to Shirley Temple nowadays," she said. In the infrequent moments when she did talk of her childhood, she referred to her experiences impersonally, as though they had all happened to someone else. As Charlie Chaplin had always called his famous tramp character "the little fellow," Shirley spoke about "that little girl." She said, "I look upon the me of those days as my little sister—I know her very well, but not as myself." Unawed, she classed herself with Rin Tin Tin. "People in the Depression wanted someone to cheer them up," she said, "and they fell in love with a dog and a little girl."

However, there was fondness in her recollections. She insisted she loved every minute. "I don't think anybody had the kind of happy existence that I had," she remarked, and one can believe she was absolutely sincere. There was no reason for her to be regretful. Her parents had invested virtually all the money she had earned, making her independent for life.

And, more importantly, she had come out of her incredible journey, with all its potentially harmful psychological risks, with only one heartbreak and emotionally healthy.

It was no small victory. Jackie Cooper, remembering his own traumas vividly, even at sixty three, said in his Los Angeles home, "Few if any child stars escape with their emotions unscarred. That Shirley Temple did was a rarity, and quite wonderful for her. As for me, I had a lot of other things the other kids did not, other experiences and money, but I grew up without the normal competition those kids had which makes them strong enough to meet the ordinary competitions of life, scholastically, sexually, whatever. I was forty years old before I got rid of all the hangups and became a truly mature adult. I count myself lucky at that. Look what happened to some of the other child actors. Look at Judy Garland. . . ."

Diana Serra Cary, Baby Peggy of the movies, writes: "With rare exceptions, all of the [movie] children . . . including [myself], suffered such severe psychological traumas as a consequence of our early careers that most of us were obliged to seek professional help in some form before we could begin to function as emotionally stable adults."

If Shirley, at thirty, was on an even keel, Baby Peggy, who was one of Hollywood's earliest and youngest child stars, admits that at the same age she "desperately needed help and guidance." Peggy, who began her career at twenty months, was a big box-office draw in the early 1920s. When she turned thirty, divorced and living in Hollywood, she could not even bear to hear "Baby Face," the song associated with her movie and vaudeville appearances. When the opening bars blared from a restaurant jukebox, she would bolt out the door and run several hundred yards sobbing in hysteria—"as though pursued by a nameless terror I could not escape." Leaving Hollywood, Peggy found solace in the Catholic Church, changed her name and married Robert Cary, an artist and art historian. After living for ten years in Mexico, she could remark feelingly, "I can easily understand how Deanna Durbin found happiness in an obscure French village."

Unlike Baby Peggy, Shirley suffered no terrors; neither did she want or need the kind of seclusion to which both Deanna and Mrs. Cary retreated. Like them, she turned her back on Hollywood and the motion picture colony and chose to settle in upper-class suburbia.

In 1954 when Charles went to work for the Stanford Research Institute, the Blacks moved to Atherton, a small exclusive community some thirty miles south of San Francisco. Her third child, Lori, was born April 9 of that year.

The ranch-style home she and Charles bought on a quiet side street was set on an acre of land, had twelve spacious rooms, a swimming pool, a large garden and a patio laid out in random-size green concrete rectangles, with strips of redwood in between. Adjoining the pool was a little house in the shape of a carousel, with a circular wooden sun deck and a carved merry-go-round horse at the entrance. Shirley picked up the horse in a San Francisco antique shop and worked on it for months, scraping it to the bare wood, sealing the saddle and harness and repainting it pure white.

The only reminders of the movie child were in a few bits of

memorabilia. The desk and chair she had used in her studio bungalow at 20th Century were in her son's room. Stored away were albums containing the scripts and photographs of her films. And, of course, she had her doll collection. These all belonged to another era; this one belonged to family. "The real thing is to be happily married and rearing children," she said. "That's what every woman wants, isn't it?"

Unquestionably, it was what Shirley wanted at thirty, and ever afterward, and she devoted herself totally to the task. The centerpiece of what she called her "full and overflowing life" was, simply, motherhood.

In her second marriage she had found the permanency in human relationships she once had in her parents' home, when all the Temples had gathered around the dinner table and Shirley, the star, was just the kid sister. She had loved that kind of warmth and closeness, which had been missing from her movie life and, sadly, her first marriage.

During her motion picture years, her associations with people were evanescent; friends made during the making of a film ended when it was completed. Acquaintances remained, but few lasting bonds were formed. When the next movie was begun, new people entered, then slipped away as the others had done.

None of this, of course, implies that Shirley was not popular with the Hollywood set. On the few occasions that she returned she was greeted with enormous affection by those with whom she had worked. But there is a gulf of difference between the people one knows and intimate friends.

Now, in her home, husband and family, she had, at long last, relationships that were solid, deeply rooted and durable, as they had been in Santa Monica and Brentwood. It was what she had wanted all along, and she guarded it almost fiercely. Her children—Linda Susan was ten, Charles Junior six and Lori four—were strictly off limits to reporters and photographers who came calling, and Shirley herself granted interviews only rarely.

Any action which she felt was an attempt to exploit her children outraged her. One pointed example of this had occurred several years before in Washington, when Linda Susan was attending an exclusive private school in Bethesda. One morning Shirley read in the *Washington Post* that her daughter would be making her "stage debut" in a class play, a pantomine of "Cinderella." The newspaper published a photograph of the little girl in her costume along with a picture of Shirley when she was about the same age.

Shirley, bristling with anger, accused the school of trying to "commercialize on me and my daughter" by arranging for publicity and pictures. She withdrew Linda Susan from the play, and from the school as well. "My only desire is to be retired and left alone," she said.

A brouhaha resulted. Donald W. Honeywell, headmaster of the Honeywell School, denying any attempt at commercialization, said Shirley had brought her daughter's costume to the school the day before and had even helped pose her and the other children for the newspaper and a national magazine. Shirley called this and other statements by the school "an absurd line of defensive drivel . . . I did what any mother would do if her baby girl were about to be exploited by publicity-hungry adults."

She stood her ground, having no regrets despite what she called "the wintry blast of publicity."

When her son was six months old, she refused to have him christened in a church because, she felt, the pastor wanted to show him off to the congregation. She had requested a private family ceremony, but the clergyman insisted on having the baby christened along with some twenty others so that the parishioners could stand in the doorway and watch. "You must realize, my dear," the pastor told her, "that you will always be watched, wherever you go, whatever you do, because you will always belong to the public."

"And my baby?" Shirley replied. The baby was christened elsewhere.

There was no lack of money. Shirley had her millions; Black too was independently wealthy and, moreover, was a highly paid executive at the Ampex Corporation in Redwood City, a ten-minute drive away. Still, their lifestyle was astonishingly simple.

Shirley was again doing all of the food shopping, most of the housework and a lot of the gardening and was cooking three and sometimes four meals a day. She employed only one woman, part time, to help out and baby-sit, and a professional gardener came once weekly.

Believing that family intimacy was nourished by a general participation of all hands in household chores, she insisted that everyone pitch in. And they did. Linda and Charles Junior made their own beds and did them over if they weren't right, spruced up their rooms and kept their clothing neatly in their (regularly inspected) drawers and closets. Even Lori was drafted to do what she could. Charles was no sit-by-the-fire lord of the manor, either: he would often barbecue their dinner and clean up afterward, and could handle a vacuum cleaner and a floor waxer efficiently.

In her kitchen, Shirley kept a recipe file, the entries clipped from newspapers and magazines. In her bedroom, she kept a scrapbook whose pages were totally unlike her old autograph book with its celebrated names. Into it she pasted homemade birthday cards and other mementos of a family growing up.

Her codes were, in the best sense of the term, hand-me-downs from her mother and father. She lived by the same kind of straight-line morality they did, and raised her children with their style of old-fashioned orthodoxy that coupled love, understanding and a no-nonsense strictness.

She believed in disciplined freedom for her children, independence coupled with responsibility. Thus, when Susan was barely three, she was permitted to play outside and find her own fun, but was instructed to return to the house at a specified time. Unable to read, she was given a watch and told that when the big and little hands arrived at a certain point on its face, she must be at the door. Susan never overstayed her limit.

The children were not only permitted but encouraged to express themselves. Sometimes their observations were overly candid. When Shirley agreed to do a television special, *Beauty and the Beast*, Charles Junior told his mother, "Gee, you'll make a nifty beast." Lori was even more candid. When a photographer from a national magazine came to take a picture of the family after the TV program was announced, she informed him, "Mommy has a big wide bottom."

Television was rationed to no more than two late-afternoon hours daily, the programs carefully edited to screen out violence and fear-provoking fare. Movies were no big deal with any of the Blacks. When they were young, the children were permitted occasional Saturday matinees at the local cinemas and, rarer still, Shirley would go into a storage cabinet, choose one of her own films and show it at home.

Her standards for movies were undeviatingly strict. Once she was the mother in charge of escorting Lori's class to a film. In the first few moments, they witnessed the horrendous death of parents in a car accident and the serious injury of their children and the family dog. Shirley rose from her seat and hustled the youngsters out of the theater. On the way out, she bawled out the manager of the movie house, then went home and dashed off an indignant letter to the producer.

Dinner was a family affair, a ritual conducted almost exactly as it had been when George and Gertrude presided at their table years before. It was served shortly after 6 P.M. Each child was included by the age of two. And free-wheeling discussions on any subject from puppy dogs to politics, Bach to birds, were encouraged, with each family member taking a turn as "chairman."

Fan letters to Shirley had dwindled to a trickle, and the secretaries to answer them were gone. Nor did she have any publicity agent or business manager. All calls came to her directly, and she turned down all offers except for interior-decorating jobs. As a licensed professional, she was developing a thriving business in the community. But she chose her assignments with care; as soon as she became aware that a client wanted to gossip about the movies, she marched off.

She worked, too, in a variety of volunteer jobs. Closest to her heart was the Multiple Sclerosis Foundation. Ever since age twenty-nine she had been a member of the national board, and she would soon become chairman of the organization's Hope Chest campaign, coordinating the work of some 125 chapters. There was a reason for her interest.

In 1950, when he was only thirty, her brother George had contracted the incurable disease, which affects the nervous system and

155

can cause severe disability. The Temples were anguished: George, a strong young man who had served in the Marine Corps during World War II, soon was confined to a wheelchair, able to walk only with the aid of two aluminum canes. Shirley has never ceased being active in the foundation's work to stimulate research to find the cause and a cure.

One day each week, patients coming to a clinic for emotionally disturbed children in nearby Palo Alto would have their case histories taken, prior to treatment, by Shirley. Another day, Shirley would put on her pink-lady uniform and help patients prepare for discharge at the Stanford University Medical Center on the university grounds in Palo Alto. She also delivered blood samples to the lab and wheeled new mothers and their babies to waiting cars. On other days, she worked as a saleslady at a shop run by a convalescent home, at a center for chronically ailing children, at a rehabilitation center for the handicapped.

As she neared her thirtieth birthday, the world of show business, which had receded further and deeper into the background, suddenly and unexpectedly once again became a part of her life.

A producer named Henry Jaffe succeeded where many others had failed, luring her back. Jaffe, who had won acclaim for his television productions of *Jack and the Beanstalk* and *Peter Pan*, was seated next to her at a dinner one evening and told her about a new TV series he had in mind, tailored expressly for her. It would be called *Shirley Temple Storybook* and would consist of dramatizations of the best-known, most-loved children's stories of all time. She liked the idea. "I'm a pushover for fairy tales," she said.

After a number of telephone discussions, Shirley's enthusiasm increased. Then one evening at dinner she put the subject, quite literally, on the table, and the question— to return or not to return before the cameras—was debated at a family council session. It was Lori's turn to preside and, despite the importance of the issue before the house, she was not passed over. The pros and cons were batted around. There was general agreement—in point of fact, wild enthusiasm on the part of the children—that Mommy should go back. Mommy pointed out that if she did so, and performed herself in all of the shows, it meant she would have to remain in

Hollywood for long periods of time. This dampened their ardor somewhat. Finally, as is commonly done in legislatures, a compromise was reached. Mommy should go back but act in only a few of the shows, narrating the rest. This would keep her away only about one day a week.

Shirley communicated the sense of the house to Jaffe, who dispatched an associate to arrange a contract.

Whether by nature or nurture, or both, Shirley at thirty had developed a finely honed sense of business. When Jaffe's associate arrived, she rolled a sheet of paper into a typewriter and tapped out a one-page contract calling for a flat fee plus a percentage of the profits. She and the associate signed it and the deal was on. Jaffe, reading it later, commented, "I'm a lawyer, but if I needed a lawyer I'd take Shirley." Later an enlarged agreement was drawn up, but it did not differ appreciably from the one Shirley had written.

Her business shrewdness manifested itself in another way. Shirley got on the telephone to the Ideal Toy Company, asked to talk to Ben Michtom and told him about her reentry into the entertainment world. It would, she said, be a good time to reissue the Shirley Temple doll. Michtom agreed enthusiastically, and when the series began thousands of little dolls, this time with vinyl and plastic faces and bodies, were in the toy stores, royalties flowing to the real Shirley. A few years later, when she entered politics, a Shirley Temple doll joke went the rounds: You wind it up and it runs for Congress.

Shirley flew to Los Angeles in February 1958 to rehearse for the opening show, *Beauty and the Beast*. She spent virtually all her time at NBC, rehearsing, and at the Beverly Hills Hotel, studying her script and waiting for the nightly call from home. In *Beauty* she performed only as narrator; Charlton Heston and Claire Bloom played the transformed prince and the lovely princess. Heston, just off his success as Moses in *The Ten Commandments*, declared himself happy to have another elaborate makeup to hide behind.

The show drew huge ratings and was a big hit with critics and audience. However, as the series progressed, interest waned. Of the sixteen programs, Shirley acted in *Mother Goose* and the final one, *The Legend of Sleepy Hollow*; then she went back to Atherton.

The series was notable for the show-business debuts of Shirley's children, which were not moments to be treasured by either the audiences or the young performers. Linda Susan, Charles and Lori were badgering their mother to get into the act, and finally she agreed to let them, but not because she was interested in starting them on theatrical careers. "I wanted them to learn that acting is hard work," she said, "that in show business nobody gives you something for nothing."

The three came down to Hollywood to appear in *Mother Goose* and spent the day under the hot lights playing the roles of village youngsters. In the wardrobe room, Lori complained that her costume was "old-fashioned" and Charles balked at the makeup they put on his face. Charles had just one line, which he didn't utter to the satisfaction of director Mitch Leisen. Perched atop a maypole, he was supposed to say, "I see him coming! It's the prince, the prince!" He gave the line with about as much enthusiasm as announcing the arrival of the milkman. Leisen asked Shirley if she could get him to put more excitement into it. Charles looked down and replied, "I'm getting tired sitting up here, Mommy." Shirley told him, "You're the one who wanted to be on TV."

San Francisco and Shirley's own community took the shows in stride. When the series premiered on television, one newspaper headlined the story "LOCAL SOCIALITE STARS ON TV." After a number of the shows had been televised, Shirley attended a Ladies' Aid Society meeting at which the chairperson announced, "Girls, one of our number is doing something very fine in the dramatic line and I want to introduce her to you." Shirley started to rise to receive approbation. But the chairperson continued, ". . . and she played so well the principal Spanish girl in the Atherton Fire Department's fine production of *Naughty Marietta*." Shirley slunk back into her seat.

Dedicated as she was to personal privacy and domesticity, it is surprising that she would venture back several times more into the unprivate world of entertainment, in which managing a home and family was not an easy matter. In 1961 she became the hostess and occasional actress in another fourteen-program series, *The Shirley Temple Show*, which, like its predecessor, retold children's stories.

She sang and danced in *The Dinah Shore Show, The Red Skelton Show* and *Sing Along with Mitch* and hosted a two-hour local program in San Francisco called *Young Americans on Stage.* Late in 1964, she agreed to do a series for ABC producer James Komack called *Go Fight City Hall,* in which she played the role of a social worker crusading for reforms. She journeyed down to 20th Century–Fox to make the pilot and met old acquaintances there by the score, including her old tutor, Frances Klampt, who was still teaching young actors and actresses.

The series was unable to find a sponsor, and Shirley Temple's first career, acting, sputtered out. Her second, family woman, was going strong. A third lay just ahead.

Part Three
THE WOMAN SHE BECAME

14

The Lollipop *Runs Aground*

In August of 1967, after a dinner of roast lamb and browned po-
tatoes, the Blacks held another council session. The family was
now living in Woodside, seven miles southwest of Atherton, in an
area that afforded more privacy and where it could stable the two
horses that had been added to the menagerie that already included
three cats, three dogs and assorted birds.

It was Shirley's turn to preside. She posed a question that startled the children: "Should Mommy run for public office?"

Many have wondered about that question. Why, indeed, did
Shirley Temple, the one-time legendary child star, at this point in
her life an apparently contented housewife, turn to public life?

For Shirley, the transition was natural, and even logical. She was
thirty-nine, her family almost grown. An overly qualified volunteer, she began seeking a larger, more significant outlet for her
energies than sitting on boards and working in clinics, no matter
how worthy the cause. By the early 1960s she began drifting,
though slowly, into Republican politics.

She had gotten a taste in Washington and had liked the flavor.
Several times she and Charles had been inside the White House as
guests of President Dwight D. Eisenhower; Vice-President Richard

Nixon and his wife Pat had also been hosts to them. During the early 1960s she participated in a number of fund-raising receptions, dinners and other events for the Republican Party. In 1964 she and Charles actively supported the Presidential candidacy of Arizona Senator Barry Goldwater, and the senatorial race of Shirley's former co-star George Murphy. From then on, she became increasingly interested, increasingly active.

Acting, she felt, was a "great life." However, she added, "I feel when one becomes an adult, it is a little harder to be an actress or actor because it's kind of a juvenile thing to do unless you're a Sir Laurence Olivier."

There is always an impelling force for action, a trigger that sets a course in motion. In Shirley's case, it came in 1967, when she was spending a good deal of time lecturing to affluent persons, many near retirement, urging them to become active in community and public affairs. As she traveled and talked, the thought became increasingly insistent: Why not practice what she was preaching?

"My turning point came because I had to do what I was trying to persuade others to do," she said, "get involved."

The trigger was followed very quickly by opportunity.

In June, Representative J. Arthur Younger, an elderly conservative Republican who had been sent to Congress from the Eleventh District for fifteen years, died of acute leukemia. A special election to fill his unexpired term was scheduled for November. In the weeks following Younger's death, no fewer than a dozen potential candidates announced their intention to seek the nomination. Among them was a handsome, much-decorated former Marine, Paul N. (Pete) McCloskey, Jr., forty years old, who called himself a "small-time lawyer" from Portola Valley.

By July, Shirley had made up her mind that she too would be one of them, subject of course to family approval. On the evening of the council session, the question was debated by Susan, who was nineteen and a student at the University of Oregon, Charles Junior, fifteen, and Lori, thirteen. "Do it, do it!" Lori urged, and everyone else agreed.

So she did.

It would be, they decided, a family affair. Charles Senior would

164

serve as her campaign manager and write her speeches, a dual activity he was soon to find more complex than he had bargained for. Linda Susan, on leave from the university to recuperate from mononucleosis, would take another semester off to help. And the others would stuff envelopes and do whatever else was necessary at campaign headquarters.

On August 29 she announced her candidacy officially.

Promptly at 9:30 A.M., accompanied by her husband and three children, she came into the Winchester Room of the Villa Chartier Motel in the city of San Mateo. Facing her were a dozen television cameras, several tables of newspaper reporters, and a huge group of enthusiastic supporters who cheered her repeatedly, as partisan an audience as she ever had in the old days.

Completely at ease in a matching coat and dress of bright orange and a double-strand jade necklace, she opened a twenty-six-minute press conference by reading from a four-page prepared speech.

She told the assemblage that Representative Younger had suggested last Easter Sunday that she run for the office, as he "would not be around forever." "I assured him I would give the matter serious thought," she said. "Then, as you know, Congressman Younger passed away in June."

Shirley then launched into a blistering attack on the Johnson Administration. "The Great Society, a pretty bad movie in the first place, has become a Great Flop," she declared.

She accused President Johnson of "playing politics" with the Vietnam War and said she wanted to play an active part in getting the country "back on the road of progress."

"It is not progress for the largest, strongest military power in the world to be mired down in an apparently endless war with one of the smallest and weakest countries in the world," she said.

"It is not progress when pornography becomes big business and when our children are exposed to it. It is not progress when some of our young people are so uninspired by our present leadership that they reject society, turn to drugs and become so-called 'hippies.'"

Throwing the conference open for questions, she dimpled and smiled, traces of her childhood charisma coming to the fore. Her supporters cheered and clapped, making so much noise that newsmen complained they could not hear her remarks. "This is not a rally, it's a press conference," an irate reporter chastised Shirley's backers.

Was her biggest challenge the fact that she had been a child actress and people still remembered her as little Shirley Temple?

"Little Shirley Temple is not running," she snapped back.

But in just a few days it became evident that she could not separate herself from little Shirley Temple. For worldwide media attention, suddenly and sharply, was focused on San Mateo County. Reporters arrived from the Associated Press International, the *Washington Post, Time, Life, Newsweek,* even the *London Daily Mail.* Even *Variety* dispatched a representative. Television crews flew in from France, Germany, the Netherlands, England and Sweden. Later, Chet Huntley and David Brinkley came to the sunny peninsula to follow the campaign.

Often, when she appeared in public, strains of "On the Good Ship *Lollipop*" were heard. One of her opponents, Democrat Roy Archibald, a San Mateo city councilman who had skippered a PT boat in World War II, commented, "The campaign may shape up as PT 53 versus the Good Ship *Lollipop*." Shirley herself helped dredge up her movie past when she changed her voter registration from Shirley T. Black to Shirley Temple Black and authorized car bumper stickers and buttons reading simply, "Shirley."

She asked Bing Crosby, a resident of nearby Hillsborough, to serve on her financial committee. Crosby, who was not even registered to vote, added his name to the voting polls and appeared with Shirley at a $100-a-plate dinner in the Thunderbolt Hotel. The two led the assemblage in singing the national anthem.

Shirley's views reflected a conservative, upper-middle-class outlook, although she was to say later that she considered herself to be "liberal to moderate on domestic issues and very liberal internationally." She favored taking conduct of the Vietnam war from civilian control and giving it to the military and suggested that mining Haiphong Harbor would shorten the conflict.

In a discussion of race riots, which she said she preferred to call "social unrest," Shirley likened them to childish tantrums. "You give that child some candy to stop it and the tantrum will stop. But then that child, seeing he got by with it, determines to have another." At kaffee klatsches and afternoon teas she came out against high taxes, big government, pornography, crime, and excessive noise from San Francisco Airport, located in a thickly populated area of San Mateo County. She advocated severe penalties for those guilty of violating narcotics laws.

The image which came across was that of a mother hen seeking to guide her charges along a puritanical path—a portrait of the grown Shirley that had been fixed in the public mind exactly a year before, in October 1966, when she announced her resignation as a director of the San Francisco Film Festival because the selection committee had chosen without a preview a movie she called pornographic.

The film, *Night Games,* was a Swedish entry to be shown for the first time in the United States, and had already been condemned by the *L'Osservatore Romano*, the newspaper that speaks for the Vatican. The movie, directed by Mai Zetterling, told the story of a man whose sexual relationship with his wife had been harmed by a seductive mother, and it contained some blue scenes. Shirley told fellow members of the film selection committee that it contained a preponderance of and needless emphasis on erotic detail. The committee outvoted her and accepted the film, and she quit. A few days later, tickets went on sale for the festival, and, as might have been expected, *Night Games* drew whopping audiences. Shirley had made her point, which she stuck to ever after. "In all candor," she said when the dust of the incident had cleared, "my reaction to the film was not outrage or disgust. It was sadness. It is a melancholy thing to witness what I regard as the debasement of childbirth and sex, high estates to most, including me."

Shirley was denounced as a square; her "effulgent moralism and political conservatism," wrote *The Nation*, "captured the hearts of many well-to-do matrons of San Mateo County." Conservative she was; she knew that. But if she was "square," she pointed out, she was in good company. D. H. Lawrence, whose 1928 work *Lady Chatterley's Lover* was banned for three decades, was a staunch foe of pornography, which, he wrote, he would censor "rigorously."

167

Shirley cited his remark, "You can recognize it by the insult it offers, inevitably, to sex, and to the human spirit."

Actually, Shirley's action in the *Night Games* has been widely misinterpreted. She had not called upon the selection committee to censor the movie because it was dirty, nor in fact did she censor it herself. Her opposition to government and official censorship, whether on the subject of miniskirts or movies, had been clearly stated. She had asked the committee to view the movie and decide if it met the festival's artistic standards. Her own belief was that, as "pornography for profit," it simply wasn't worth showing.

Shirley's position was backed by the *San Francisco Examiner*'s motion picture critic, Stanley Eichelbaum, who termed it a "courageous" stand, although he pointed out that her public resignation boomeranged by making the movie even more tempting to filmgoers.

Still, the incident slotted Shirley in the public mind as a prude, despite her vigorous denial that, like many women, she was "round, not square."

When local politicians personally canvass a neighborhood, they are generally greeted politely, diffidently or impatiently, depending on the degree of interest voters have in them or how busy they may be at the time of a drop-in visit. With Shirley, it was different. When she rang a doorbell one morning in Daly City, a woman answered, stared at her and blurted, "Oh Jesus!"

It was like that all during the campaign. She was, to begin with, the only woman in a crowded field, but she had instant recognition. When she appeared in shopping centers or at the gates of industrial plants or went door to door, she was followed by youngsters clamoring for autographs and incredulous housewives dazed to find her on their front steps.

Her usual costume for politicking was sensible flats, a tweed skirt, blouse and cardigan. Generally, she was accompanied by only an aide or two. She would smile, say a few words of greeting and ask for support, but it was doubtful if many really heard. All too often, the sight of her was an acute reminder of the passing years. Typical was the reaction of one woman: "That's *Shirley Temple!* I don't believe it. I feel as old as God's younger sister!"

At Half Moon Bay, a small coastal community, Shirley, dressed in a brightly striped knit dress, began a typical day meeting with a dozen campaign workers in the living room of the retired mayor. After coffee, she was driven to the high school to present awards for the best costume at the Halloween party. As she entered the gymnasium, the high-school band inevitably greeted her with "On the Good Ship *Lollipop.*" Smiling, Shirley told the assembled crowd that "the Good Ship *Lollipop* is now in the drydock." Then, accompanied by her aides, she visited the shops along Main Street, where the store windows contained red, white and blue posters with her picture, a rather mature-looking woman wearing a simple dark dress and double strand of pearls.

Shirley also went to Washington, where Senator Murphy took her to the office of Senate Minority Leader Everett Dirksen for a picture-taking session. Dirksen said if she came to Congress he would invite her on his television show. "We'll call it the Ev and Shirley Show," he chortled. As she left, they kissed and the cameras flashed.

"My husband's in California, how can I explain this?" Shirley queried, with a smile. "I wouldn't explain it," Murphy advised.

As the election neared, the Vietnam War dominated all the other issues. Shirley refused to debate her views with the other candidates, eliciting criticism both from her opponents and from the press. Four days before the election date, however, she agreed to host a debate with four of her Democratic opponents. In the interest of "party unity," she said, she excluded the other Republicans who were running.

At the event, held in a high-school gymnasium before about two thousand persons, most of whom came solely to see her, Shirley appeared with her own cheering section, a group of young girls with red-white-and-blue sashes. The girls distributed red balloons to the audience. The popping of the balloons as the evening progressed and the intermittent cheers of "S-H-I-R-L-E-Y, Shirley!

169

B-L-A-C-K, Black, Shirley Black!" and "Go, go, Shirley!" gave a show-business patina to the proceedings.

Opening the discussion, Shirley again attacked Johnson's conduct of the war and asked, "How can you say stop the bombing when a case can be made that it hasn't really started?" Her statement drew the ire of Edward M. Keating, an Atherton lawyer and a former publisher of *Ramparts* magazine, who declared she was "more to be pitied than censured for her opinions."

"I feel Mrs. Black and I live in two different worlds," he mused.

By election day, November 14, the consensus was that Shirley Temple was far ahead although Pete McCloskey and Edward Keating had strong support. Soon after the polls opened at 7 A.M., Shirley and Charles Black drove to the Redwood City polling place to cast their ballots. After voting and posing for pictures—most news coverage still centered around Shirley—they drove back to Woodside. It was a bright, sunny day and County Clerk John Bruning forecast a voter turnout of about sixty percent.

In the Black living room, where they were joined by friends, relatives and some campaign aides, Shirley and her husband turned on a television set and a radio to keep abreast of the latest returns. A cameraman and representatives of several national magazines were permitted to record the day's events.

The polls closed at 8 P.M., and fifteen minutes later the early returns gave McCloskey an initial lead. By 9 P.M., it was apparent that the old movie magic which had given Shirley instant recognition during the campaign had failed to win the election for her. In the end McCloskey was ahead by a wide margin, a total of 52,882 votes against 34,521 for Shirley. Archibald, the leading Democrat, had 15,069. Since no candidate had received a majority of the votes cast, McCloskey and Archibald would face each other in a runoff election.

Shirley had failed to carry even her home precinct!

Accompanied by her husband and children, she drove to the Villa Chartier Motel, where she had officially opened her congressional race, to concede the election. More than four hundred supporters had decorated the room with red-white-and-blue bunting and a huge campaign banner bearing her campaign slogan, "Let us work to create, to build, to inspire." Now they waited quietly as Shirley, ten television cameras trained on her, mounted the platform.

In a simple speech in which she congratulated the winners and thanked her family and supporters, she evoked memories of a plucky, determined little girl who was going to make everything come out all right.

"I will be back," she promised. "I am dedicating my life to public service because the country needs us now more than ever before and I want to help."

The next day, throughout the country, newspapers recorded the "sinking of the Good Ship *Lollipop*."

A Talk with Her Campaign Counselor

By this time, Charles Black was no longer Shirley's campaign manager. He was replaced by a professional political public-relations organization, Whitaker & Baxter, the California firm whose clients had included Earl Warren, Richard Nixon and Dwight D. Eisenhower. Whitaker & Baxter hired Victor Gold, a Washington newsman and public-relations consultant. Gold later worked for Vice-President George Bush in the 1980 campaign and prior to that was press secretary for Vice-President Spiro Agnew. He was also a press assistant for Barry Goldwater when he ran for the Presidency, and in 1967 he entered the Shirley Temple Black campaign as an "imported East Coast PR gun—on for $2,000 a month plus expenses."

Gold, a slim, handsome man with silver-gray hair, explained why he thought Shirley lost.

Victor Gold: "She was too much the lady. She had a tough opponent in McCloskey. I knew that immediately and I tried to get her to go for his throat, but she wouldn't do it. She believed in that damned Eleventh Commandment, the Parkinson edict that California Republicans love: Don't speak ill of any Republican candidate.

"You know, all politicians are actors; they have to be. But, despite her background, Shirley Temple Black could not and did not play that role. The problem with Shirley as a campaigner reflects to her credit as a person—although it is a discredit if you want to be an elected official.

"One morning I picked her up at her home in Woodside. The day's schedule included a stop at a manufacturing plant in Redwood City, a luncheon, a meeting that night. The agency had sent a car for her, and Shirley climbed in the front beside the driver. I got into the back.

"The conversation was pleasant, but she was very emphatic about one thing especially; she was going to keep her family life separate and intact, and her children would have their privacy. The campaign must not interfere. That meant she was going to be home at six-thirty every night for dinner with her family. Well, you can't really run a campaign like that. You have to be more flexible.

"We pulled into the parking lot in the rear of the plant, and almost immediately she was surrounded by workers who poured out of the factory to see her. I was amazed. I've never seen anything like it. I've gone around with candidates, but nobody ever got that kind of greeting. They really identified with her.

"She met people very well on a personal basis. She shook hands, she was wonderful, one to one. She told them she was running for office and asked for their help.

"Still, I always felt there was always something aloof about her. They couldn't see it, but, watching her, I could. This came out more strongly when she spoke before crowds. She came across as rigid, highly principled and cordial, but with little flexibility.

"Her speeches were no help, either. Black wrote them. He's a very fine and civic-minded person—they both are—but he knew nothing about politics. He's an engineer. He would get advice from Cap Weinberger and some of the people up in Sacramento. Then he'd write those long, dull speeches and she'd read them, pages and pages. That night at the Thunderbird she had the audience stupefied.

"Before I came on, they had taken public-opinion polls which showed Shirley had a ninety-eight percent recognition factor. That's marvelous for a candidate. But polls also showed that only twelve percent of the people said they would vote for her, six percent would vote for McCloskey and another twelve percent was divided among the other candidates. The public did not translate that recognition factor into Shirley as a credible congressman. We could not change that."

Shirley has never run for office again and has said she never intends to enter another race. Years later she called her sole experience "a circus."

"We had thirteen candidates, twelve men and Shirley," she quipped. "It sounds like an old Deanna Durbin movie, doesn't it?"

Election night, when it was all finally over, Stanley Hiller, her honorary campaign chairman, told her she had two choices: "you can either go home and close the door or you can get on the road and help your party." Shirley chose the latter course and was the star attraction at fund-raising dinners for the Nixon campaign in twenty-two states and forty-six cities.

In August she went to Vienna for a meeting of the International Federation of Multiple Sclerosis Societies, of which she is a founder, and then to Prague to discuss Czechoslovakia's participation. On the evening of August 21, after meeting with the Minister of Health and neurologists and bacteriologists studying the disease, Shirley returned to her suite in the Alcron Hotel to get her luggage together. The next morning she was to leave for home. At about midnight, she listened to the news over Radio Prague and then retired for the night, dimly aware as she slept of the noises of low-flying jet planes.

She was awakened by a loud knocking on her door. "Awake, madame!" she was told. "We are invaded!" During the night Russian soldiers had taken over the airport, and tanks had rolled into the city streets. U.S. Embassy officials sent word to Americans at the hotel—there were some four hundred geologists and tourists in Prague—to remain inside until arrangements could be made to evacuate them.

Throughout the day Shirley could hear the sounds of scattered gunfire, explosions which shattered windows, and fire trucks rushing to the scene of blazes. That night Embassy personnel picked up the Americans, formed a convoy of a hundred private automobiles, preceded and followed by official Embassy cars, and escorted them safely through Russian roadblocks into West Germany.

At home she resumed her work for the Republican National Committee and was sent back to Europe—Rome, Paris, Frankfurt, Brussels and London—to urge Americans living abroad to vote by absentee ballot and to contribute to the party coffers. In all, Shirley helped raise almost a million dollars for the 1968 campaign, a feat which many felt was responsible for her designation the following year as a United States delegate to the twenty-fourth General Assembly of the United Nations.

Although the appointment was greeted with some astonishment, she was not the first celebrity to receive it. U.S. delegations had traditionally included a popular figure who could bring publicity to the United Nations. Irene Dunne, Myrna Loy and Marian Anderson had served as delegates. And, as it proved, Shirley was a most felicitous choice.

When the ten-member delegation, headed by Ambassador Charles W. Yost, was sworn in on September 16, 1969, cameramen, as they had done all of her life, focused on Shirley Temple Black, becomingly clad in a brilliant red suit, her brown hair pulled back in a French twist. When she arrived at her office on the seventh floor of the U.S. Mission the first day, news photographers were waiting. And so it went throughout the thirteen-week session.

Veteran diplomats asked for her autograph and mentioned their favorite Shirley Temple movies. United Nations employees brought their children to meet her. And she was always pointed out by the guides shepherding tourists through the building. One reporter said she and Miss Angie Brooks, the Liberian president of the Assembly, shared honors as "the ranking celebrities" of the session.

It soon became apparent, however, that she took her appointment very seriously. Active and hard-working by nature—she had been employed since she was three, as she often pointed out— Shirley did not want to be a mere figurehead. She rose early and made her own breakfast in the kitchenette of her suite in a New York East Side hotel. Then she descended to the lobby, her red patent-leather briefcase with a big "N" (for Nixon) tucked under her arm, and picked up her bodyguard for the short ride to the U.S. Mission at United Nations Plaza. A New York City detective accompanied her everywhere, upon the insistence of the State Department, after threats had been made on her life.

Yost had assigned her to committees dealing with the environment, youth, refugees and the peaceful uses of outer space, and she set out to prepare herself thoroughly. She spent many hours reading background material on United States policy, researching and writing her own speeches and attending the many committee meetings and sessions.

As might have been expected, her lack of experience in diplomacy led to some beginner's mistakes. On one occasion, she found herself, without advisers, on the receiving end of searching questions by Soviet delegates about "airborne sensing techniques." Not willing to admit that she was unfamiliar with the subject she filibustered. "I told them everything I knew about outer space that wasn't classified—which wasn't the answer to their specific questions by any means," she says.

She was criticized for not voting one day despite specific instructions to do so by her government, and also for making statements without prior consultation with U.S. allies.

Her speeches, marked by short, forceful sentences, evoked mixed reactions. The Tanzanian delegate admiringly remarked, "They are not written in governmentese." Other delegates found them oversimplified and trite.

She began a speech on the refugee problem with a somewhat unorthodox discussion of American treatment of the Indians. She was particularly interested in the problems of the Indians, she told the delegates, because "Cherokee blood flows proudly in the veins of my own son and daughter." (Husband Charles is a descendant of General John Sevier, first governor of Tennessee, who was married to a Cherokee princess.) While her words received the approval of Ambassador Jamil Baroody of Saudi Arabia and others on the refugee committee, members of the U.S. Mission were somewhat appalled by her frank criticism of American actions.

However, as the session continued, she became extremely skillful at the diplomatic negotiations which were carried on constantly in the halls and corridors of the United Nations, at the luncheons and the dinners. Glen A. Olds, U.S. representative in the Economic and Social Council, later called her "the U.S.'s secret weapon." And Representative Dante Fascell, who was also in the delegation, told her, "You took over even more than your share of the burden."

At night, Shirley either worked in her hotel suite or attended one of the many social events on the UN calendar. Many weekends she flew home to be with her family, and Black once a month came East to join her, on one trip carrying in his luggage an urgent package.

Shirley had been sitting at her desk one evening, writing to him, when she felt a furry object brush her leg. She thought it was a mouse, but the telephone operator to whom she reported it said, "There are no mice in this hotel, it must be a rat." An engineer searching under her bed with a flashlight confirmed that a rat had just crawled into a hole. Shirley, as capable as she had ever been in a movie, added a postscript to Charles to bring a large trap from the cellar. He did and the problem was solved.

The Assembly finished its work in December, and Shirley, who had thoroughly enjoyed her taste of diplomacy, said she hoped she would get another chance. She suggested that the five members appointed by the President serve for two years, the first as an alternate to gain experience and the second as a full delegate. She also wrote personal notes to both the President and Secretary of State Rogers asking for another international assignment.

Nixon did not follow through on that suggestion, but he did name her deputy chairman of the U.S. delegation to the UN preparatory committee which was to plan for an international conference on the environment in Stockholm in 1972. Chairman of the committee was Christian Herter, Jr., whose father was the secretary of state in the Eisenhower Cabinet. John D. Ehrlichman, White House counsel, was one of the delegates.

In April 1971, Egyptian delegates to the UN invited Shirley to visit their country and meet President Anwar el-Sadat, who had been in office barely six months. She was having tea with Jihan el-Sadat, swapping pictures of children, when "in the door walked this handsome Egyptian gentleman wearing gray flannel pants and a blue blazer."

Flustered, Shirley dropped her purse, and its contents, passport, money and lipstick, spilled on the floor. Sadat helped restore her belongings, and the two discussed some of her movies. He asked for, and Shirley later sent, his own print of *Heidi*.

Sadat gave her a "secret" message for President Nixon, Shirley said. "Tell your President, I am the first Arab leader to truly want peace."

She relayed the message to Nixon's secretary, Rose Mary Wood. "Rose Mary apparently didn't think it was substantive, because she didn't tell Nixon," Shirley says.

In June she delivered the final speech of the Stockholm meeting, stressing the urgent need of nations to cooperate in solving environmental problems. In July 1971, in Belgrade for an international law conference, she flew with the delegation to meet with Marshal Tito, the Yugoslav dictator, at his luxurious home on the island of Brioni in the Adriatic Sea. At lunch, Tito gave instructions that she be placed next to him. When they were seated he told her, "I did not believe I would be sitting next to Shirley Temple, whom I remember from the movies when I was much younger." Shirley, aware Tito was scheduled to come to the United States that fall for an official visit with President Nixon, invited him to visit her at her home. "I'll cook a dinner for you." she said. "Sure," Tito replied, but his schedule was too tight and he never got to collect Shirley's promised home-cooked meal.

Then President Nixon appointed her special assistant to the chairman of the President's Council on Environmental Quality. She was preparing to attend a Moscow conference when she had to make a fateful decision.

177

15
Mastectomy: "Don't be afraid."

The little girl who made world news with a spell of illness at ten created headlines once again when she became sick at forty-four. But this time, it was much more serious.

On Friday, September 1, she was sworn into her new post at the Executive Office Building; then she returned to her two- room suite at the Jefferson, a small, elegant Washington hotel only four blocks away, packed and flew home to Woodside and a reunion with Charles. The next morning, she slept a little later than usual, took a luxurious bath and made what she expected to be a routine self-examination of her breasts.

Ever since her middle twenties, she had followed the advice of her gynecologist faithfully, checking herself in between regular office visits, particularly following menstruation. She knew that it was not possible to overstress the importance of this brief personal test.

For two decades, she had noticed nothing. But this time, there *was* something different. She felt a small lump on the upper portion of her left breast.

She did not panic. She had never been a scary child and she had not become a fearful grown-up. She did what she knew had to be done, quickly and methodically.

She telephoned her doctor and went for an examination. It included a mammography, the special X-ray study that can detect tumors that are small or deeply hidden in the breast tissue, and supply additional information on a growth's shape and density. Mammography is more accurate than inspection and palpation, but less so than a biopsy, the surgical removal of a small portion of tissue for microscopic testing.

When the examination ended, the doctor put the odds as three chances in five that she had only a harmless cyst. At the same time, however, he suggested she have the biopsy performed.

A long and heavy schedule of important work lay ahead. After the conference in Russia, there would be a symposium in Cincinatti organized by the U.S. Environmental Protection Agency. Scientists and civic leaders from all across the nation would attend, and Shirley, deeply committed to the cause, wanted to be there. Lacking what she later called "any sense of urgency" about the lump, she and the surgeon made an appointment for the following November 2 for the biopsy.

In Moscow the first doubts came.

She began to feel some pain, not a great deal, but there had not been any before. There was a strange burning, too, in her left breast which stirred ominous thoughts. "I bet this isn't going to be good," she said to herself in her hotel room one morning.

All through her stay, the feeling that she might have a serious problem nagged at her but she pushed it to the back of her mind. After she affixed her signature to the environmental pact the delegates had agreed upon, setting forth the rights and obligations of countries and individuals to safeguard the purity of their living space, she delivered an address in which she said, "We all have to learn how to survive. We can live." The remark was more prophetic than she knew at the time.

Back in the States, she read all she could find on breast cancer, and finally told Charles. On Wednesday morning, November 1, she packed a small overnight bag and drove alone through the gently rolling hills, glowing in fall coloring, to the Stanford Univer-

sity Medical Center fifteen minutes away. She parked, and unrecognized, walked past the broad lawn, bordered by eucalyptus,
pine and cypress trees, through the double doors of the hospital's
west wing. After the usual interrogation at the admissions office,
she checked into her room, number 106, just off the long wide
corridor.

It was hardly VIP quarters; there are none at the center. Measuring seventeen by twelve feet, it had soft beige walls, a gray speck-
led linoleum floor and a single bed stuck in the middle. The tall
windows looked out on the lawn, in the center of which was the
hospital's pride, a fountain spouting water fifty feet high.

The next morning, in the surgical suite on the floor above, Dr.
Frederic P. Shidler performed an incision biopsy. Before she was
taken upstairs, Shirley had made it clear what she wanted: she was
authorizing only a biopsy. Nothing more at this time. If the verdict
went against her, she insisted on the right to decide for herself the
nature and extent of any further surgery.

The report from pathology was not bad, but neither was it good.
The entire tumor, measuring just under an inch in diameter, had
been removed. Most of it was benign, but a small fragment at one
end showed evidence of malignancy.

Charles, waiting in the room, was told the news. When Shirley
was brought down, she was still somewhat groggy from the anes-
thetic, but dry-eyed and stoical. Susan, then twenty-four, and Lori,
eighteen, were at the house, waiting for the report. Shirley called
them and asked them to come to the hospital. (Charles Jr. was
thousands of miles away, on a ship somewhere off Central America, a crew member of a fishing vessel.)

Quickly the two girls jumped into a car and hurried to Room 106.
Once again, the Blacks held a family council about a major change
in their lives.

Controversy, often impassioned, still exists over the question of
how much the surgeon should remove when breast cancer is
diagnosed.

Proponents of radical mastectomy, the traditional operation for
more than eighty-five years, insist that the best cure rates are
achieved by removal of the breast, the chest muscle beneath and

the axillary lymph nodes in the chest and armpit. These nodes are a primary route for the invasion of the rest of the body by daughter cells. Some doctors advocate an even more radical procedure, removal of other lymph node chains in the area of the breast which are located inside the chest. Still others feel that the patient would be served best by removing the remaining breast as a precaution, even though it does not appear involved, because in at least ten percent of the cases a new malignancy occurs there. (This happened to Happy Rockefeller and to Ingrid Bergman.)

On the other hand, advocates of conservative surgery claim that good, and possibly even better, results have been obtained by removal of the breast alone—a "simple" mastectomy—followed by radiation treatment of the lymph nodes.

The advantages and disadvantages of the various procedures were explained to the Blacks. Shirley's own doctors recommended a modified radical, removal of the breast and several lymph nodes but leaving the chest wall and muscle intact. Still, the ultimate decision was Shirley's.

At that somber family gathering in Room 106, Shirley explained the medical findings and her options. Susan and Lori embraced their mother and wept with her.

All that day, Shirley pondered the choices. Finally she decided on the modified radical, reasoning—with a heavy dose of fatalism—that if an invasion had already taken place the extended radical would probably not be in time anyway.

Next morning, shortly before eight, Shirley was transferred to a stretcher once again, wheeled into the broad corridor by an orderly and taken by elevator for the second time to the surgical suite one floor above. She was put into one of the thirteen operating rooms in the suite and placed under the bright lights. Dr. Shidler, gowned and masked, came in to greet her, and a moment later the anesthetist appeared at her side.

Charles remained in her room, waiting. He had brought about a dozen photographs from home which he put up around the room, pictures of Shirley as she was now, of their children, and a few of little Shirley in her famous starring roles. He had also brought a batch of knicknacks, little reminders of home, to soften the stark simplicity of the hospital room for Shirley.

Assisted by a resident and an intern, Dr. Shidler removed the breast and a few lymph nodes. The surgery took only one hour, and Dr. Shidler, who is now retired, recalls that Shirley awoke as soon as she was removed to the recovery room.

"She was a little groggy but just fine," he said at his home in Menlo Park. "I went downstairs to her room, where Mr. Black was waiting, to tell him the surgery had gone well. He too was fine. Both had reached a stable emotional position, knowing that the breast had to be removed. They had accepted that, and so neither displayed a great deal of emotion afterward."

In the early afternoon, young Gary Cavalli knocked gently on her door. Gary, twenty-three and just a year out of Stanford, was the hospital's assistant information officer. He had been assigned to handle press relations, which the administration expected to be a tough job as soon as news leaked out that Shirley Temple Black was a patient there.

Gary was surprised to hear Shirley call out in a strong voice, "Come in." He was more surprised when he saw her.

"Before I went in there," Cavalli recalled, "I thought to myself, 'She's probably all worn out. Bet I find her pale, groggy and in a lousy mood. But there she was, sitting up, smiling and greeting me with a cheery 'Hi, how you doin'?'

"Charlie Black was with her, and he was bustling around the room, making things comfortable. I told her there were sure to be requests for interviews, in fact some had already come in—you don't keep things long from the press and television around here— and I fully expected her to put them off at least a little while. Instead she said. 'When do you want to do them?' She was incredible."

On Monday, three days later, the phone rang in the office of Dave Shutz, managing editor of the *Redwood City Tribune*, Shirley's local newspaper. Shutz, who had known Shirley a long time, took the call even though it was only a few minutes before deadline.

"That was the day before the Presidential election," Shutz recalled, "and the tension was higher than usual. Shirley told me she was in the hospital and asked if I could come down to see her that day. There was something special she wanted to talk to me about. I told her I'd be there after the paper went to press.

"A few minutes later, I left the office and drove to the medical center. Shirley was sitting up in bed, Susan at her side. She told me she wanted to convey an important message to all women. She explained that she had had breast surgery on Friday and that she wanted me to deliver the story to the newspapers and wire services, stressing that it be told fully, simply and accurately. She wanted nothing hidden.

"What she wanted most was to send a message of hope to women, and that others facing the same operation should not have fears about it. That it's not the end of the world. That she still had a full life to live in every way. That there is not only hope but no reason at all to despair. 'Tell them I'm feeling just great,' she said, 'that I have no fears about my recovery and that I expect to be back on my feet, doing everything I ever did before, in a few days.'"

Shutz gave the story to the world.

"After that," Gary said, "the phones never stopped ringing. The media people jammed every square foot of space, and I can't tell you how many people, nurses and doctors among them, slipped me pieces of paper to get her autograph.

"And flowers! It looked like a whole florist's shop had been moved in there. She sent them to other floors, the children's wing, everywhere. Gifts and messages came from all over the world. It was a wonderful tribute. People cared; they cared a whole lot."

Later, Shirley had a press conference at her bedside at which she amplified what Shutz had reported.

Wearing a coral negligee and a white gardenia above her right ear, she told reporters from the press, radio and television that she had undergone surgery for the removal of a cancerous breast. It was the first time a celebrated person had openly discussed an operation that all women dread and, until then, few had made public. Later, First Lady Betty Ford and Mrs. Rockefeller, following her lead, also publicized their mastectomies widely.

Shirley had shown the way. "The only reason I am telling this," she said at the conference, "is because I fervently hope other women will not be afraid to go to their doctors when they note any unusual symptoms. There is almost certain cure for this form of cancer if caught early enough.

"I am grateful to God, to my family, and my doctors for the successful outcome of this operation because I have much more to accomplish before I am through . . ."

Shirley admitted it was hard to accept the surgery psychologically but, "You don't let vanity get in your way." She smiled and the dimples showed. "It's not so bad," she said.

Shirley's courageous statement won the admiration and respect of the press and the medical authorities. In an editorial titled "Shirley's Warning," a California newspaper wrote: "She could have retreated into privacy. Instead, Mrs. Black allowed her case to be publicized on television and in the newspapers."

Dr. Shidler: "Her candor about a serious, much-dreaded problem was a milestone in helping other women deal with a similar illness. When she came forward the way she did, she showed other women that by meeting the situation openly, they too, and their loved ones, can face it much more clearly than if it were concealed.

"Just as importantly, after Mrs. Black had come forward with her statement, many women who would not otherwise have done so came to their doctors for examinations. I myself saw a great many patients who sought checkups because of the way Mrs. Black had met the problem. Other doctors told me the same thing. "She did a remarkable thing, a valuable thing."

Before she made her press announcement, Shirley had been receiving an average of 350 letters and telegrams a day. Afterward, the total leaped to well over a thousand a day. The medical center received so many requests that Stanford issued a special report on breast cancer.

The following week, Charles took Shirley home. "They left by the main entrance, like everybody else," Gary said. One month later she was living her same full life.

16
The Ambassador

Shirley was attending the Law of the Sea Conference in Caracas, Venezuela, in late August 1974 when reporters asked her to confirm a story just announced by the government of Ghana that President Ford had selected her as ambassador from the United States.

She had not yet been told by Washington of the appointment, so she suggested the press check the White House. Then she quickly placed a call herself to Secretary of State Kissinger seeking to nail down the "rumor."

"It's not a rumor," Kissinger told her. "It's a fact. And you know why? Because you asked me about Namibia. I know you will do well over there." He was referring to a conversation in 1969 when he was briefing delegates to the UN Assembly, and Shirley, he said, asked insightful questions about Namibia's problems.

Not everyone was so sanguine about the appointment. Yale Professor David Apter, an expert on West African politics, termed it "irrelevant and outrageous." Hollywood columnist Joyce Haber wrote, in amazement, "Shirley Temple? Ghana? Gee whiz! As if we didn't already have enough troubles abroad."

Shirley herself contributed to the dismay with an enthusiastic but unfortunate comment that she had read in an encyclopedia that Ghana exports most of the world's chocolate. "I just love chocolate," she added ingenuously.

There were also mutterings that the appointment was a political payoff, she was asked by a reporter how much it had cost. After the Senate approved her appointment, Shirley (saying that Senate rules had prevented her from answering before) said she and Black had contributed a total of $1,167 in the past four years to Republican campaigns, with only $307 going to the national campaigns.

Then, with the customary Temple dedication and discipline, she proceeded to do her homework. She participated in fifty-five briefings, studying Ghana's history, economy, climate and mores. In December, accompanied by her husband and her daughter Susan, she moved into the two-story residence of the American ambassador in Accra, the capital of Ghana. Charles and Lori, at school in California, would join the family at holiday and vacation times.

Ghana, lying just north of the Equator on the west coast of Africa, is largely a matriarchy. Women manage the farms, own the fishing boats and run the taxi fleets, so a lady ambassador aroused no feelings of resentment. As a matter of fact, Shirley's smiling, easy manner and free-wheeling approach to diplomacy, which disregarded much of the stuffiness, delighted the Ghanaians.

One sultry ninety-degree day soon after her arrival the ambassador, dressed in a colorful cotton African-print dress, a matching head scarf covering her head, visited the Makola Market, an open-air bazaar in the center of Accra where clothes, food, jewelry and spices are sold in closely packed stalls.

The market women cheered and reached out to touch her, the boldest even hugging and kissing her. Smiling gaily, she returned their greetings in native Fanti, Ga and Twi. Before she left, Shirley, who could always pick up a dance step easily, delighted the market women with an impromptu "highlife," Ghana's traditional dance.

It was soon apparent that Shirley Temple Black was a hit. "She has proved herself to be a capable, wonderful person who is determined to work for the good of others," editorialized the *Ghanaian Times*. The *Echo* called her "an astute diplomat."

She was made an honorary *aboutsendomhene* (deputy chief) of the Fanti tribe by its principal chief, Nana Mbra V, who renamed her Nana Shirley Temple Black I. Another powerful, and usually very aloof, chief, Asantchene Otumfue Opoku Ware II, leader of the Ashanti tribe, came to call at her residence and also granted a private audience at his palace in Kumasi, capital of the Ashanti region.

The ordinary Ghanaians loved her, too. Months after her arrival birth registries were reporting that babies were being named after her, even boys.

Her day began early. She arrived at her teak-walled embassy office by 7 A.M. and often returned home with barely enough time to change to formal dress for a diplomatic reception. In the intervening hours, seated at a massive desk which almost dwarfed her, behind her the American flag and the ambassador's flag, she supervised with crispness and efficiency the activities of the seventy-seven-member embassy staff and the 175 Peace Corps and Agency for International Development personnel assigned to Ghana.

Many visitors to her office were American businessmen seeking information about investment opportunities in Africa. Shirley helped them make the proper contacts. She also inaugurated monthly discussion meetings with American and Ghanaian representatives of the thirty-five American companies operating in Ghana. As time went on, she became very outspoken about the need to assist in the economic development of the African countries.

"I'm all in favor of investment—getting something back—but in today's world there has to be more reciprocal advantage, mutual benefit, in our relationship with developing countries," she said.

Susan accompanied her on several trips to get a firsthand picture of American operations in Ghana. On one trip, they helicoptered to the Firestone rubber plantation and tire factory at Bonsaso, a small village several hours away. Another day, they had to put on safety goggles and hard hats for an inspection tour of a smelting plant operated by the Kaiser Aluminum Chemical Company and the Reynolds Metal Company at Tema, a port city.

Shirley enjoyed the diplomatic social scene and made effective use of the skills she had honed at the United Nations to develop personal and cordial relations with other diplomats. She paid a courtesy call at the Chinese Embassy, where she was served tea and lichee nuts. When the Chinese ambassador returned the call, Shirley served a typical American treat—chocolate M & Ms. Some weeks later, at a Ghanaian party, she opposed him at a rollicking table-tennis game. He won. Later she also lost at chess to the counselor of the Soviet Embassy.

She was exceedingly informal most of the time and once offended some American visitors by appearing in a robe and sneakers and chewing bubblegum. On the way out, one of the visitors remarked somewhat cattily, "I'll never forget you as Dorothy in *The Wizard of Oz*."

The Black family adapted well to life in Ghana. To cope with the intense tropical heat, Shirley had a pool built behind the residence. Charles Black found Ghana a convenient home base between travels for his food development projects, and both he and Susan accompanied Shirley to many diplomatic functions.

Susan, twenty-seven, long-haired, leggy and bearing a strong resemblance to John Agar, was much sought after by younger members of the diplomatic corps, particularly darkly handsome Roberto Falaschi, the thirty-three-year-old first secretary of the Italian embassy in Ghana.

In 1975, the Blacks went back home to Woodside for a short visit so that Susan could be married to Falaschi in a candlelight ceremony at the Valley United Presbyterian Church.

Ambassador Black's informality gave way to strict professionalism in October 1975, when 150 picketers marched and shouted outside the embassy in opposition to American aid to Angola. Watching from a window, she did nothing. "I understand dissent in America," she said. However, when one of the demonstrators began to lower the American flag she quickly dispatched an aide to raise it again.

She liked her job and was somewhat chagrined a few months later when Secretary of State Kissinger came to Africa with a message from President Ford. The President wanted her to come to Washington as chief of protocol. There were reports that her first reaction was negative, but Ambassador Black denied this. "Obviously when the President asks you to do something you do it," she declared. She told the Senate Foreign Relations Committee considering her appointment on June 22, "I'm energetic. I'll work hard and I look forward to shaking up anything I see that needs shaking up." The next day, by voice vote, the Senate confirmed the appointment.

She was sworn in on July 20, 1976, as the country's first woman chief of protocol, with the dual rank of ambassador and assistant secretary of state. Her predecessor, Henry E. Catto, Jr., went to Geneva to be the United States representative to the European office of the United Nations.

Shirley got right to work. That night, at a diplomatic reception, "I introduced four hundred people I didn't know to the President," she says.

The Blacks sublet an apartment on Massachusetts Avenue which Shirley filled with furniture, carpets and drapes from her homes in California and Ghana. She eschewed most social engagements except for the necessary official functions, preferring to cook dinner for herself and her husband and spend a quiet evening at home. Charles Black operated his Mardela Corporation from a Washington base, as he had done from Ghana.

Among the duties of the protocol chief is to take total charge of visiting heads of state, including advance planning for the visits, greeting them at the airport and shepherding them to all events until they leave. Sometimes being the first woman in the job presented problems.

Protocol dictates that a distinguished guest go through the doorway first. But when Shirley called for Urho Kekkonen, President of Finland, to escort him from Blair House to the White House, he would have none of that. Steeped in Old World courtesy, he indicated that ladies should go first, and he waved her on. Shirley, sticking to the edicts of the State Department, demurred. Finally, a compromise was reached and they went through the doorway together.

"By the time we got to the White House we were a neat team,"

Ambassador Black says. "In the case of skinny doors, we went through sideways."

At another reception, Shirley went after a wandering head of state who seemed to be looking for something. "You don't hover, but you always stand nearby," she explains. Somewhat embarrassed, he confessed he was looking for a man to direct him to the bathroom.

Treasury Secretary William E. Simon precipitated a controversy with a request that he be permitted to keep gifts he had received from foreign officials and governments during his travels abroad. A 1966 law requires that such gifts, if valued at fifty dollars or more, must be turned over to the government for display or auction. However, Simon wanted his gifts as mementos and wrote to the protocol head offering to pay the government the appraised value, which, he said, would be more than could be recovered at auction. The gifts included a watch from Leonid Brezhnev, a Russian shotgun, a set of matched pistols from Argentina, two necklaces from Israel, a cigarette box from Saudi Arabia and a porcelain sculpture from Spain.

Ambassador Black, as stern with transgressors as in the old days, wrote to Simon that granting his request would violate the spirit as well as the letter of the law. She said it would not be fair to others who might have turned in gifts they wanted to keep.

A compromise was reached, with four of the gifts becoming the property of the U.S. government. Three of them, the Russian shotgun, the watch and the pistols, at Simon's suggestion, were put on display at the Treasury Department. The cigarette box went to the State Department for display or disposal. Simon was permitted to keep the necklaces, worth less than fifty dollars, and the sculpture, a personal gift from the Spanish minister.

The end of Shirley's tenure at the State Department was signaled when Jimmy Carter won the election. He did not ask her to stay on the job. She remained in Washington to arrange for diplomatic attendance at the inauguration and to introduce the diplomatic corps to the new President. Then she returned to her Woodside home.

17

Profile at Fifty-plus

In April of 1981, three months after the inauguration of Ronald Reagan as the fortieth President, Shirley Temple Black flew to Washington and checked in at the Jefferson Hotel. She ordered dinner sent to her room, retired early and by 8:45 the next morning was entering the vast State Department Building on C Street N.W., in Foggy Bottom. After showing her credentials at the desk, she walked briskly down the corridor at the right to Room B, a large chamber some forty feet long and twenty-five feet wide. Its severe, businesslike appearance was only slightly softened by the beige-carpeted floor and the brown striped drapes on the windows. The furniture, businesslike square tables, was arranged in a large rectangle. A blackboard, several sticks of chalk on the ledge, had been set up in a corner.

Already a dozen persons were seated at the tables, notebooks in front of them. Shirley nodded to them, took her place at one of the tables and arranged her own notes. Others drifted in; by nine the tables were filled with newly appointed United States ambassadors and their spouses who were about to leave on their first overseas missions. They were prestigious lawyers, heads of large corporations, former high political officials and others of like stature, coming to be briefed by Shirley Temple Black.

These three-day orientation sessions, which are sponsored by the Foreign Service Institute, an arm of the State Department, are intensive courses on the day-to-day management of an embassy, the handling of local personnel, the resources available and anything else a new envoy needs to know about his or her job. Shirley, who receives a small fee for her services, shares the chair with Dean Brown, an old friend who was ambassador to Jordan and Senegal and is a former undersecretary of state.

The seminars are private; no outsiders and no media representatives are permitted to attend. Says Evan Press, who sets up the seminars for the Institute, "Just watching Mrs. Black is part of the education. She is very professional, gracious, diplomatic, businesslike. There is no trace of the movie star of the old days, except in her smile. Of course, everybody recognizes her and remembers her movies, but there is no talk of that. She has a great time at the seminars, and so does everybody else."

In June of 1981, Maxwell M. Rabb, a distinguished attorney who was secretary to the Cabinet in President Dwight D. Eisenhower's Administration, sat and listened to Shirley before going off on his assignment as ambassador to Italy. Anthony Quainton, the new ambassador to Nicaragua, attended the December briefings.

On one trip, Shirley almost literally bumped into George Murphy in Washington. He was on his way to visit clients of the consulting service he runs, and she was en route to the State Department. "We talked about the old days," Murphy recalled, "and she complained jokingly that I took too long to teach her the last routine in *Little Miss Broadway*."

On the last day of the sessions, a long one which ends at about nine in the evening following a reception attended by the Secretary of State, Shirley returns to her hotel and packs. Next morning, she flies home.

She lives in one of the country's wealthiest residential areas, the town of Woodside, which lies on the eastern slope of the Santa Cruz Mountains, halfway between the Pacific Ocean and San Francisco Bay. There are no industries in Woodside, only orchards and estates on its rolling terrain, all with sweeping lawns and mansions hidden behind tall trees and shrubs. Old-line society, with its old money, is concentrated here. It is the home of the northern-California horsey set, where stables are an even more highly rated status symbol than foreign cars. As might be expected, Woodside is largely conservative politically and, as someone remarked, a hotbed of social rest.

Like the others, Shirley lives in understated affluence on her three-acre estate. Her home, a two-story Tudor-style building of brick and stucco, is almost invisible behind its screen of interlocking pines and red-berried pyrocantha. Outside, across Lakeview Drive, is a row of six mailboxes, one of them hers, but there are no names. Inside, the home is beautifully furnished, but not palatial. In the blue-and-cream living room, to the left of the entry hall, are a number of African artifacts, mementos of her service in Ghana. French doors beyond the dining room open into a terrace at the back of the house, where Shirley and Charles host receptions. Beyond is a rectangular swimming pool. A garage has been converted into a spacious pool house, which is also used as a family playroom. A large marlin hangs on one wall; on another is "Gumpus Ozus," a silly-looking animal from the NBC production of *The Land of Oz.*

She and Charles are empty-nesters now. Susan has begun a family of her own. In December 1980 a baby was born to the Falaschis at Stanford Medical Center. Roberto had to be away on business for his government, and Shirley remained with her daughter during labor and watched the delivery of her first grandchild, Teresa Lyn. Shirley wasn't surprised, but the public apparently wasn't as ready as she was. Typical was the reaction of Londoners, duly recorded by the *Daily Express:* "Shirley Temple a granny? Incredulous fans shrieked." But she is and, like all proud grandmothers, carries the baby's picture in her wallet.

Charles Junior, who studied international law, and Lori, a photography student, are out of the house, too.

George and Gertrude are gone now. They had lived at the Willow Creek Apartments in Palo Alto since 1967; then, in 1974, they made their home with Charles and Shirley in Woodside. On December 29, 1976, Gertrude fell ill and was taken to the Stanford Hospital, where, on New Year's Day of 1977, she died at the age of eighty-four. It was her sixty-fourth wedding anniversary; George was with her every moment she was in the hospital. On September 30, 1980, George Temple passed away at Shirley's home at the age of ninety-two. Spry as ever, he played golf at the Los Altos Golf and Country Club until shortly before his last brief illness.

When we telephoned Shirley one day in spring, Charles answered. "Shirley is unable to speak right now," he said. "She's busy cooking dinner." Thanks to roots planted by Gertrude, she is as domestically minded as ever, and as well organized. Up at six-thirty, she starts her day by arranging her calendar of activities. There may be meeting of the many groups to which she belongs, visits to friends, a variety of social activities and, certainly not least, the marketing and the shopping.

She and Charles will drive to the shopping center in the center of town to browse in the garden center, pick up some things at the drugstore, then walk across the road to Robert's Market. Charles will push the cart, and the Blacks will wander through the aisles. She is a careful shopper, buying only what is necessary, rarely on impulse.

Shirley drives her own Jaguar, a sporty two-seater, and still does most of her own cooking. Luncheon guests have learned not to expect anything fancy; when Dave Shutz, the newspaper editor, came for lunch one day, Shirley fixed tuna sandwiches.

At fifty-plus, Little Shirley may be buried in the past, but there are unmistakable similarities to the tot of the movies. "Like everyone else," she says, "I've grown a little bit wider—and a little bit wiser." But if the child is gone, the quality is still pure Shirley. The vivacity, the eye action, even some of the gestures are sharp reminders. Little Shirley used no makeup before the camera, because her skin glowed with health. Big Shirley's skin is as remarkably pink and clear as ever, and she uses no creams or lotions.

There are similarities that go deeper than appearance and manner. The Shirley of the movies had a code. She was fair-minded, gutsy and, above all else, passionately honest. Today's Shirley is perfectly aware that the stories of her films were fictional pap, but, because she played her roles in the most impressionable period of her life, the simple lessons they taught have remained with her. So when she believes in a cause, there's no mistaking where she stands. She was a hawk during the Vietnam War and, head up, did not waffle on her points. When faculty members joined in student protests on college campuses during those turbulent years, she did not like it one bit and said so. When the women's liberation movement gathered force, she said she preferred "the strong arms of my husband around me"; besides, she made it plain she herself had been liberated "at the age of three when I started working." She was criticized for the solid, stolid conservatism that these and other stands represented, but she did not quail. Little Shirley never backed down, either.

When Little Shirley gave her word, you could be assured she kept it, come what may. Big Shirley is equally straightforward, dealing honorably with people on all levels. A typical instance is recalled by Harry Farrell, a reporter for the *San Jose Mercury* who is also a friend:

"Shortly after the election of Richard Nixon, a story came over the Associated Press wire that he might appoint a woman to a post in his Administration. Shirley's name was mentioned as a possibility. I got on the phone to her at once and asked her. After all, that was big news here and everywhere.

"She told me frankly she knew nothing about the report, that nobody had said anything to her about it. That was that, I figured. Just before hanging up, I tossed off a line: 'Well, remember if anything happens who asked you first.' She answered that if anything did, I would be the first to hear from her.

"I forgot completely about the incident. On Christmas Day, I was home in the middle of the afternoon having dinner with my family. The telephone rang. It was the operator at the newspaper. I have an unlisted number at home. 'Shirley Black is trying to reach you,' the operator said.

"What on earth for? I wondered. And why in the middle of Christmas afternoon? I called her at once. She was at home. She told me she had just gotten word that the United Nations job was indeed in the works and that someone might leak the story of her appointment to other news media. She said she remembered that she had promised me six weeks earlier I would be the first to know if anything happened. She was keeping her word, knowing how important an exclusive story like this is to a newspaperman.

"I hung up, rushed down to the paper and wrote the story, the first to appear on her impending appointment as a member of the U.S. delegation to the United Nations."

Little Shirley was accustomed to long hours of hard work. Big Shirley has never been busier. She is on the board of directors of three corporations, the Fireman's Fund Insurance Company, Del Monte Corporation, and the Bank of California and its parent company, BanCal Tri-State Corporation. She serves also as a director or active member of at least eight other national organizations. She receives more than a thousand requests for speaking engagements a year, but accepts only a few.

She has kept her resolve never to go back into show business. "I am happy to serve in the real world," she says, "not the world of make-believe." In 1977, she made a brief "sentimental journey" to Hollywood to receive the Louella O. Parsons Award of the Women's Press Club there for presenting "the best image of Hollywood to the world."

However, her abiding interest now lies in the field of international affairs. She travels extensively, mostly on business for her organizations. In 1981 alone, she went to Europe four times, once on a tour sponsored by the North Atlantic Treaty Organization to West Germany, where she was impressed, and horrified, by the bristling Soviet military might aimed at Western Europe.

In 1977, when she and Charles were guests of the People's Republic of China, the pupils at a dancing school in Peking begged her to show them some of the steps she did in her movies. She breezed through the routines she had done with Bill Robinson in *Rebecca of Sunnybrook Farm* almost forty years ago.

She does not resent these reminders, knowing that the memories of her as a movie star are useful ice-breakers. "Little Shirley opens up doors for Shirley Temple Black," she says, but adds, "If big Shirley can't produce, the doors close." She drew the line, however, when, giving her views on Chinese policy to a distinguished San Francisco audience, she was asked to sing a chorus of "On the Good Ship *Lollipop*." Ever the seasoned diplomat, she turned down the request with virtually the same words she had used on a similar occasion at Westlake.

In 1974, while the Arab oil embargo was in force, she obtained a private audience with Egyptian President Anwar el-Sadat, who gave her a message to pass on to President Richard Nixon. "I will lift the embargo," he told her. "I will lift it for President Nixon." Nobody knows, of course, what part memories of the moppet played in softening up Sadat, but it's a good bet they helped.

Fifty years after it began, the Temple phenomenon continues. Temple artifacts, whether they are dolls, toys, buttons, pictures, postcards or cereal bowls, are tracked down and quickly snapped up when they are offered for sale. The market is so large that several books describing the collectibles that are available have been published. In Anchorage, Alaska, a thirty-nine-year-old librarian and mother of two, Jackie Musgrave, publishes a bimonthly newsletter, the *Collector's News*, informing subscribers in the United States, England, Holland, Australia, South Africa and New Zealand of the latest offerings and sales. Many dealers have files of people who are interested in Shirley material, and notify them as soon as items turn up.

Fan clubs celebrate her birthday. On her fifty-third, large groups in Whittier, California, Tekonska, Michigan, and elsewhere met, sang "Happy Birthday" to her and demolished huge pink cakes, then watched Temple movies, swapped Temple memorabilia and told Temple stories.

Ted Menten, a Manhattan author, collector and designer, says the Temple doll is the "single most sought-after celebrity doll ever." He has several hundred Shirley dolls, of about twenty thousand, in his own collection. Two years ago on a television show preceding a doll auction in Texas, Menten displayed an eighteen-inch Temple doll in the *Stand Up and Cheer* costume. The doll was in perfect condition, in the original box, and had the signed photograph that came with every doll. "Within a few days," he recalls. "I had offers for it from all over the country." Early eighteen-inch composition dolls, he says, can be sold for $500 to $1,000 depending on the condition.

Little Shirley always tried to make things come out right for everybody, crusading in her determined way to cure the wrongs she saw in life. With her deep interest in world affairs, especially problems of the Third World countries, the environment and the eradication of the disease that struck down her brother, Shirley Temple Black is crusading still.

The ultimate goals and the personalities may be different, but the feisty Temple spirit and the intensity she summons up to the tasks have not changed, nor will they ever change.

A Shirley Temple Filmography

In her early film appearances, Shirley Temple played lead and bit parts in the following series of one and two-reel comedies.

War Babies (Educational Films, 1932). *Cast:* Shirley Temple, Eugene Butler, Georgie Smith. *Credits:* Producer, Jack Hays; director, Charles Lamont. This short, the first of the Baby Burlesks, satirized *What Price Glory.*

The Runt Page (Educational Films, 1932). *Cast:* Shirley Temple, Georgie Smith, Raymond Bunion. *Credits:* Producer, Jack Hays; director Roy La Verne. A spoof of the newspaper drama, *The Front Page.*

Pie Covered Wagon (Educational Films, 1932). *Cast:* Shirley Temple, Georgie Smith. *Credits:* Producer, Jack Hays; writer, Jack Hays; director, Charles Lamont. A tale of the old West in which Shirley is captured by the Indians.

Glad Rags to Riches (Educational Films, 1932). *Cast:* Shirley Temple; Georgie Smith, Eugene Butler, Marilyn Granas. *Credits:* Producer, Jack Hays; director, Charles Lamont. Shirley plays a nightclub entertainer and sings "She's Only a Bird in a Gilded Cage," her first song on the screen.

Kid's Last Fight (Educational Films, 1933). *Cast:* Shirley Temple, Sidney Kilbrick, Georgie Smith. *Credits:* Producer, Jack Hays; director, Charles Lamont. A boxer's girl friend, Shirley is kidnapped by gamblers but escapes in time to appear for the big fight.

Kid 'n' Hollywood (Educational Films, 1933). *Cast:* Shirley Temple, Georgie Smith. *Credits:* Producer, Jack Hays; director, Charles Lamont. Shirley plays a beauty contest winner forced to scrub studio floors on her hands and knees to support herself, until she gets a chance to replace the reigning star and mimic Marlene Dietrich and Mae West.

Polly-Tix in Washington (Educational Films, 1933). *Cast:* Shirley Temple, Marilyn Granas, Georgie Smith. *Credits:* Producer, Jack Hays; director, Charles Lamont. A political satire, set to music, in which Shirley vamps her way into the life of a very important figure.

Kid 'n' Africa (Educational Films, 1933). *Cast:* Shirley Temple, Danny Boone Jr. *Credits:* Producer, Jack Hays; director, Charles Lamont. A spoof of the jungle films in which Shirley, a big-game huntress, is rescued from cannibals by a Tarzan type.

Dora's Dunkin' Donuts (Educational Films, 1933). *Cast:* Shirley Temple, Andy Clyde, Blanche Payson, Florence Gill, Fern Emmett, Georgia O'Dell. *Credits:* Producer, Jack Hays; director, Harry J. Edwards; writers, Ernest Pagano and Ewart Adamson. Shirley appears in a radio show promoting a floating doughnut invented by the young proprietor of a failing bakeshop.

Merrily Yours (Educational Films, 1933). *Cast:* Shirley Temple,

Junior Coughlin, Helene Chadwick, Mary Blackford, Harry Myers, Sidney Miller, Kenneth Howell. *Credits:* Producer, Jack Hays; writer, Charles Lamont; director, Charles Lamont. Shirley plays the little sister of Junior Coughlin in the first of three two-reelers titled "Frolics of Youth."

Pardon My Pups (Educational Films, 1934). *Cast:* Shirley Temple, Junior Coughlin, Kenneth Howell. *Credits:* Producer, Jack Hays; director, Charles Lamont. The second of the Frolics of Youth series, based on the story of a spaniel, "Mild Oats," by Florence Ryerson and Colin Clements.

Managed Money (Educational Films, 1934). *Cast:* Shirley Temple, Huntley Gordon, Junior Coughlin. *Credits:* Producer, Jack Hays; director, Charles Lamont. Shirley is again the little sister of Coughlin as he attempts to raise funds for a military school.

New Deal Rhythm (Paramount, 1934). *Cast:* Charles "Buddy" Rogers, Marjorie Main, Shirley Temple. Shirley had a walk-through part in this two-reeler.

Shirley Temple appeared in forty-two full-length features in walk-on, bit and starring roles.

The Red-Haired Alibi (Tower Production, 1932). *Cast:* Grant Withers, Merna Kennedy, Theodore Von Eltz, Purnell Pratt, Fred Kelsey, Shirley Temple. *Credits:* Director, Christy Cabanne; screenplay, Edward T. Lowe. Shirley has a bit part as the daughter of a gangster. The film was based on a novel by Wilson Collison.

To the Last Man (Paramount, 1933). *Cast:* Esther Ralston, Randolph Scott, Jack LaRue, Buster Crabbe, Barton MacLane, Gail Patrick, Shirley Temple, Noah Beery. *Credits:* Director, Henry Hathaway; screenplay, Jack Cunningham. Shirley plays the daughter of Gail Patrick and Barton MacLane in this film based on Zane Grey's novel.

Out All Night (Universal, 1933). *Cast:* ZaSu Pitts, Slim Summerville, Shirley Temple, Laura Hope Crews, Shirley Grey, Billy Barty, Gene Lewis. *Credits:* Director, Sam Taylor; screenplay, William Anthony McGuire. Shirley is "checked" at the department store nursery where ZaSu Pitts is supervisor.

Carolina (Fox, 1934). *Cast:* Robert Young, Lionel Barrymore, Janet Gaynor, Shirley Temple, Richard Cromwell, Stepin Fetchit. *Credits:* Director, Henry King; screenplay, Reginald Berkeley. Shirley played the role of a sharecropper's daughter in the story based on a play, *The House of Connelly,* by Paul Green.

Mandalay (Warner Brothers–First National, 1934). *Cast:* Kay Francis, Lyle Talbot, Ricardo Cortez, Ruth Donnelly, Warner Oland, Reginald Owen, Shirley Temple. *Credits:* Director, Michael Curtiz; screenplay, Austin Parker and Charles Kenyon. Shirley made a brief appearance on a jungle steamer.

Stand Up and Cheer (Fox, 1934). *Cast:* James Dunn, Madge Evans, Shirley Temple, Warner Baxter, John Boles, Ralph Morgan, Dick Foran, Stepin Fetchit, Nigel Bruce. *Credits:* Director, Hamilton McFadden; screenplay, Ralph Spence. Shirley sang "Baby, Take a Bow" and broke into the big time in this musical potpourri based on a story outline by Will Rogers and Philip Klein.

Now I'll Tell (Fox, 1934). *Cast:* Helen Twelvetrees, Spencer Tracy, Shirley Temple, Alice Faye, Vince Barnett, Henry O'Neill. *Credits:* Director, Edwin Burke. A melodrama based on the life of gambler Arnold Rothstein, as told by his widow.

Change of Heart (Fox, 1934). *Cast:* Charles Farrell, Janet Gaynor, Shirley Temple, James Dunn, Ginger Rogers, Jane Darwell. *Credits:* Director, John G. Blystone; screenplay, Sonya Levien and James Gleason. Shirley had a small role in this film, which was based on *Manhattan Love Song,* a novel by Kathleen Norris.

Little Miss Marker (Paramount, 1934). *Cast:* Shirley Temple,

Adolphe Menjou, Charles Bickford, Dorothy Dell, Lynne Overman, Edward Earle. *Credits:* Director, Alexander Hall; screenplay, William R. Lipman, Sam Hellman, Gladys Lehman. This is the Damon Runyon story of a little girl left by her father with a gambler as security for money to play the horses.

Baby, Take a Bow (Fox, 1934). *Cast:* Shirley Temple, James Dunn, Claire Trevor, Alan Dinehart. *Credits:* Director, James Lachman; screenplay, Philip Klein and E.E. Paramore, Jr. An ex-convict (Dunn) tries to go straight for the sake of his family. Shirley (his daughter) finds the real thief of the pearls when the finger of suspicion points at her daddy. Adapted from the James P. Judge play *Square Crooks*.

Now and Forever (Paramount, 1934). *Cast:* Shirley Temple, Carole Lombard, Gary Cooper, Charlotte Granville, Sir Guy Standing. *Credits:* Director, Henry Hathaway; screenplay, Vincent Lawrence and Sylvia Thalberg, from a story by Jack Kirkland and Melville Baker. Shirley helps keep her father, an international swindler, from a life of crime.

Bright Eyes (Fox, 1934). *Cast:* Shirley Temple, James Dunn, Jane Darwell, Jane Withers, Judith Allen, Lois Wilson. *Credits:* Producer, Sol M. Wurtzel; director, David Butler; screenplay, William Conselman, from a story by David Butler and Edwin Burke. Shirley's widowed mother dies and her father's friend, an aviator, tries to adopt her. Film has Shirley singing "On the Good Ship *Lollipop*" before bailing out of an airplane in Dunn's arms.

The Little Colonel (Fox, 1935). *Cast:* Shirley Temple, Lionel Barrymore, Sidney Blackmer, Hattie McDaniel, Evelyn Venable, John Lodge, Bill Robinson, Alden Chase. *Credits:* Producer, B. G. De Sylva; director, David Butler; screenplay, William Conselman. The film takes place in the Deep South following the Civil War. Shirley helps reunite her mother (Evelyn Venable) with her grandfather (Lionel Barrymore), a grumpy colonel who disowned his daughter for marrying a Yankee.

Our Little Girl (20th Century–Fox, 1935). *Cast:* Shirley Temple, Joel McCrea, Rosemary Ames, Lyle Talbot, Erin O'Brien Moore, Margaret Armstrong. *Credits:* Producer, Edward Butcher; director, John Robertson; adapted by Stephen Avery from "Heaven's Gate," a story by Florence Leighton Pfalzgraf. When Shirley's parents decide to split up, she runs away to their favorite picnic area to celebrate a family holiday all by herself.

Curly Top (Fox, 1935). *Cast:* Shirley Temple, Rochelle Hudson, John Boles, Arthur Treacher, Jane Darwell, Etienne Girardot, Esther Dale. *Credits:* Producer, Winfield Sheehan; director, Irving Cummings; screenplay by Patterson McNutt and Arthur Beckhard. A remake of the "Daddy Long Legs" story by Jean Webster, with Shirley as the little orphan adopted by a rich bachelor.

The Littlest Rebel (20th Century–Fox, 1935). *Cast:* Shirley Temple, John Boles, Karen Morley, Bill Robinson, Jack Holt, Guinn Williams, Bessie Lyle, Hannah Washington. *Credits:* Producer, Darryl F. Zanuck; director, David Butler; screenplay by Edwin Burke from the play by Edward Peple. Shirley's father, a Confederate soldier, is captured by Union troops and is sentenced to death, so she goes to Washington to plead for clemency from President Abraham Lincoln.

Captain January (20th Century–Fox, 1936). *Cast:* Shirley Temple, Slim Summerville, Guy Kibbee, Buddy Ebsen, June Lang, Sara Haden, Jane Darwell. *Credits:* Producer, Darryl F. Zanuck; director, David Butler; screenplay by Sam Hellman, Gladys Lehman and Harry Tugend, based on a novel by Laura E. Richards. Shirley is rescued from a shipwreck and cared for by a kindly old lighthouse keeper until a mean truant officer tries to take her away.

Poor Little Rich Girl (20th Century–Fox, 1936). *Cast:* Shirley Temple, Alice Faye, Gloria Stuart, Jack Haley, Michael Whalen, Sara Haden, Jane Darwell, Claude Gillingwater. *Credits:* Producer, Darryl F. Zanuck; director, Irving Cummings; screenplay by Sam Hellman, Gladys Lehman and Harry Tugend, based on the stories of

Eleanor Gates and Ralph Spence. Shirley, the neglected daughter of a soap king, runs away and meets up with a song-and-dance team (Alice Faye and Jack Haley), only to find herself singing on the radio show of her daddy's main competitor.

Dimples (20th Century–Fox, 1936). *Cast:* Shirley Temple, Frank Morgan, Robert Kent, Delma Byron, Astrid Allwyn, Stepin Fetchit, John Carradine, Herman Bing. *Credits:* Producer, Nunnally Johnson; director, William A. Seiter; screenplay by Arthur Sheekman and Nat Parrin. Shirley conducts a band of street children on New York's Bowery and appears as Little Eva in a production of *Uncle Tom's Cabin.*

Stowaway (20th Century–Fox, 1936). *Cast:* Shirley Temple, Alice Faye, Robert Young, Eugene Pallette, Helen Westley, Arthur Treacher, J. Edward Bromberg. *Credits:* Producer, Darryl F. Zanuck; director, William A. Seiter; screenplay by William Conselman, Arthur Sheekman and Nat Perrin, from a story by Sam Engel. Shirley's parents, missionaries in China, are slain by bandits, and she is adopted by a rich playboy after she stows away on his cruise ship.

Wee Willie Winkie (20th Century–Fox, 1937). *Cast:* Shirley Temple, Victor McLaglen, C. Aubrey Smith, June Lang, Cesar Romero, Michael Whalen, Constance Collier. *Credits:* Producer, Gene Markey; director, John Ford; screenplay by Ernest Pascal and Julian Josephson from the story by Rudyard Kipling. Shirley and her widowed mother come to live with her grandfather, commander of a British army post. Shirley becomes friendly with a captive native. When he escapes and plans to attack the post, she helps settle the conflict.

Heidi (20th Century–Fox, 1937). *Cast:* Shirley Temple, Jean Hersholt, Sidney Blackmer, Arthur Treacher, Helen Westley, Mady Christians, Pauline Moore, Delmar Watson, Marcia Mae Jones. *Credits:* Producer, Raymond Griffith; director, Allan Dwan; screenplay by Walter Ferris and Julien Josephson, based on the book by

Johanna Spyri. Shirley's wicked aunt sends her off to her grand-father, an old woodcutter, and then, after she grows to love him, to the home of a rich little invalid girl. After Shirley teaches the girl to walk again, the housekeeper attempts to sell Shirley to the gypsies.

Rebecca of Sunnybrook Farm (20th Century–Fox, 1938). *Cast:* Shirley Temple, Randolph Scott, Jack Haley, Gloria Stuart, Phyllis Brooks, Helen Westley, Slim Summerville, Bill Robinson, Alan Dinehart, J. Edward Bromberg, William Demarest, Franklin Pangborn. *Credits:* Producer, Raymond Griffith; director, Allan Dwan; screenplay by Karl Tunberg and Don Ettinger, based on a story by Kate Douglas Wiggin. A very loose presentation of the story, with Shirley singing, on a radio program, many songs from her previous successes.

Little Miss Broadway (20th Century–Fox, 1938). *Cast:* Shirley Temple, George Murphy, Phyllis Brooks, Jimmy Durante, Edna Mae Oliver, George Barbier, Jane Darwell, El Brendel, Donald Meek, Edward Ellis. *Credits:* Producer, Darryl F. Zanuck; director, Irving Cummings; screenplay by Harry Tugend and Jack Yellen. Orphaned Shirley is adopted by the manager of a boardinghouse for actors. She organizes a variety show, gets a $5,000 contract and wins over the mean old lady next door who owns the building and threatens to evict the actors.

Just Around the Corner (20th Century–Fox, 1938). *Cast:* Shirley Temple, Joan Davis, Charles Farrell, Bert Lahr, Bill Robinson, Franklin Pangborn, Cora Witherspoon. *Credits:* Producer, Darryl F. Zanuck; director, Irving Cummings; screenplay by Ethel Hill, J. P. McEvoy and Darrell Ware, based on a story by Paul Gerard Smith. Shirley's father, an architect, is down on his luck and working as a maintenance man. Shirley helps convince the penthouse occupant to start a new construction project where he employs her daddy.

The Little Princess (20th Century–Fox, 1939). *Cast:* Shirley Temple, Anita Louise, Richard Greene, Cesar Romero, Ian Hunter, Arthur Treacher, Marcia Mae Jones. *Credits:* Producer, Darryl F. Zanuck;

director, Walter Lang; adapted by Ethel Hill and Walter Ferris from the novel *Sara Crewe,* by Frances Hodgson Burnett. When Shirley's father is reported dead during the Boer campaign, a mean headmistress switches her from a plush room to the attic. Convinced that he is still alive, the little girl haunts the corridors of a veterans' hospital until, with the aid of Queen Victoria, she finds her father, alive and recuperating from loss of memory.

Susannah of the Mounties (20th Century–Fox, 1939). *Cast:* Shirley Temple, Randolph Scott, Margaret Lockwood, J. Farrell MacDonald, Martin Good Rider, Victor Jory, Maurice Moscovitch, Moroni Olsen. *Credits:* Producer, Darryl F. Zanuck; director, William A. Seiter; screenplay by Robert Ellis and Helen Logan, from a story by Fidel La Barba and Walter Ferris, based on a book by Muriel Denison. Shirley, the sole survivor of a wagon train of pioneers massacred by Canadian Indians, is rescued by Inspector Randolph Scott of the Mounties, who is, in turn, captured. Her plea to the Indian chief saves his life and calms the rebellious tribe.

The Blue Bird (20th Century–Fox, 1940). *Cast:* Shirley Temple, Spring Byington, Gale Sondergaard, Nigel Bruce, Eddie Collins, Johnny Russell, Russell Hicks, Sybil Jason, Gene Reynolds, Sterling Holloway. *Credits:* Producer, Darryl F. Zanuck; director, Walter Lang; adapted by Ernest Pascal from the play by Maurice Maeterlinck. Shirley and her little brother creep from bed in their woodchopper father's home to search for the mythical Blue Bird of Happiness. They visit the fantasy world of the past and the future, only to discover the Blue Bird in their own home.

Young People (20th Century–Fox, 1940). *Cast:* Shirley Temple, Charlotte Greenwood, Jack Oakie, Arleen Whelan, George Montgomery, Kathleen Howard, Darryl Hickman, Mae Marsh. *Credits:* Producer, Harry Joe Brown; director, Allan Dwan; screenplay by Edwin Blum and Don Ettinger. Shirley, an orphan, is raised by a vaudeville couple and becomes the third member of the team. In order to give her a proper home life, the Ballantines retire to a small town, where they are treated poorly until a hurricane hits and their song-and-dance routines help cheer the populace.

209

Kathleen (Metro-Goldwyn-Mayer, 1941). *Cast:* Shirley Temple, Herbert Marshall, Laraine Day, Gail Patrick, Felix Bressart, Nella Walker, Lloyd Corrigan, Guy Bellis. *Credits:* Producer, George Haight; director, Harold S. Bucquet; screenplay by Mary C. McCall, Jr., based on a story by Kay Van Riper. Shirley is very unhappy because her wealthy father neglects her in favor of a woman obviously out for his money. Psychologist Laraine Day helps cure Shirley's troubles and ends up marrying her father.

Miss Annie Rooney (United Artists, 1941). *Cast:* Shirley Temple, William Gargan, Dickie Moore, June Lockhart, Guy Kibbee, Peggy Ryan, Roland Du Pree. *Credits:* Producer, Edward Small; director, Edward L. Marin; screenplay by George Bruce. Shirley, the daughter of a wildcat promoter with more dreams than money, receives her first screen kiss from Dickie Moore as he drives her to a party where she is snubbed by his rich friends.

Since You Went Away (United Artists, 1944). *Cast:* Shirley Temple, Claudette Colbert, Jennifer Jones, Joseph Cotten, Monty Wooley, Robert Walker, Lionel Barrymore, Agnes Moorehead, Keenan Wynn, Nazimova, Craig Stevens, Guy Madison. *Credits:* Producer, David O. Selznick; director, John Cromwell; screenplay by David O. Selznick, based on a novel by Margaret Buell Wilder. Colbert is the mother and Shirley and Jennifer are the teenage daughters in this film which depicts life on the American home front during World War II.

I'll Be Seeing You (United Artists, 1944). *Cast:* Shirley Temple, Joseph Cotten, Ginger Rogers, Spring Byington, Tom Tully, Chill Wills, Darek Harris (John Derek). *Credits:* Producer, Dore Schary for Selznick-International; director, William Dieterle; screenplay by Marion Parsonnet, based on a radio play, *Furlough,* by Charles Martin. A shell-shocked war veteran on furlough and a girl with a prison background meet and fall in love during the Christmas holiday. Shirley is Ginger's teenage cousin, in whose home the pair meet.

Kiss and Tell (Columbia, 1945). *Cast:* Shirley Temple, Walter Abel,

Katherine Alexander, Jerome Courtland, Robert Benchley, Porter Hall, Tom Tully, Virginia Welles, Darryl Hickman. *Credits:* Producer, Sol C. Siegel; director, Richard Wallace; screenplay by F. Hugh Herbert, based on his play of the same name. The film portrays the problems arising when the sons and daughters of three feuding families flirt, fall in love and even marry.

Honeymoon (RKO-Radio, 1947). *Cast:* Shirley Temple, Franchot Tone, Guy Madison, Lina Romay, Grant Mitchell, Gene Lockhart. *Credits;* Producer, Warren Duff; director, William Keighley; screen play by Michael Kanin, based on a story by Vicki Baum. Shirley flies to Mexico City to marry an American soldier, Guy Madison, but runs into diplomatic red tape which is finally straightened out by Franchot Tone, the American vice-consul.

The Bachelor and the Bobby Soxer (RKO-Radio, 1947). *Cast:* Shirley Temple, Cary Grant, Myrna Loy, Ray Collins, Rudy Vallee, Harry Davenport, Johnny Sands. *Credits:* Producer, Dore Schary; director, Irving Reis; screenplay by Sidney Sheldon. Shirley has a full-blown crush on Cary, a gay man-about-town, and sets out to snare him as an escort.

That Hagen Girl (Warner Brothers, 1947). *Cast:* Shirley Temple, Ronald Reagan, Rory Calhoun, Louis Maxwell, Dorothy Peterson, Charles Kemper, Conrad Janis. *Credits:* Producer, Alex Gottleib; director, Peter Godfrey; screenplay by Charles Hoffman, based on Edith Roberts' novel *Mary Hagen*. Shirley is an adopted illegitimate child whose life is miserable because of malicious gossip. She fails at a suicide attempt and ends up in the arms of Ronald Reagan, a much older man mistakenly thought by many of the townspeople to be her father.

Fort Apache (RKO-Radio, 1948). *Cast:* Shirley Temple, John Wayne, Henry Fonda, John Agar, Irene Rich, George O'Brien, Victor McLaglen, Dick Foran, Guy Kibbee, Grant Withers. *Credits:* Producer, John Ford and Merian C. Cooper; director, John Ford; screenplay by Frank Nugent, suggested by the James Warner

Bellah story "Massacre." Shirley's father is Colonel Thursday (Henry Fonda), a tough, bitter commander of a garrison on the Arizona frontier. The drama centers around the conflict between his law-and-order approach to handling the Apaches and that of his experienced and more genial aide, John Wayne. Film ends with powerful scenes of massacre of American troops.

Mr. Belvedere Goes to College (20th Century–Fox, 1949). *Cast:* Shirley Temple, Clifton Webb, Tom Drake, Alan Young, Jessie Royce Landis, Kathleen Hughes. *Credits:* Producer, Samuel G. Engel; director, Elliott Nugent; screenplay by Richard Sale, Mary Loos and Mary McCall, Jr. Shirley is a widowed journalism student who is writing an article about Clifton Webb, who has enrolled for a degree in order to qualify for a literary award.

Adventure in Baltimore (RKO-Radio, 1949). *Cast:* Shirley Temple, John Agar, Robert Young, Josephine Hutchinson, Charles Kemper, Johnny Sands. *Credits:* Producer, Richard H. Berger for Dore Schary; director, Richard Wallace; screenplay by Lionel Houser, from a story by Lesser Samuels and Christopher Isherwood. Shirley, a minister's daughter, shocks her father's parishioners and threatens his tenure by painting a portrait of a young man in a leopard skin and championing the cause of women's suffrage.

The Story of Seabiscuit (Warner Brothers–First National, 1949). *Cast:* Shirley Temple, Barry Fitzgerald, Lon McCallister, Rosemary De Camp, Pierre Watkin, William Forest. *Credits:* Producer, William Jacobs; director, David Butler; screenplay by John Taintor Foote based on his story "Always Sweethearts." The film is based on the career of the famed thoroughbred. Shirley is the niece of Barry Fitzgerald, the horse's trainer.

A Kiss for Corliss (United Artists, 1949). *Cast:* Shirley Temple, David Niven, Darryl Hickman, Tom Tully, Virginia Welles, Gloria Holden, Robert Ellis. *Credits:* Producer, Marcus Low, Richard Wallace and Colin Miller; director, Richard Wallace; screenplay by Howard Dimsdale, based on the Corliss Archer character of Hugh Herbert. Shirley (Corliss) writes in her diary about a fictitious romance with much married and divorced David Niven in order to make her boy friend, Dexter, jealous.   ›

Bibliography

Bacon, James. *Hollywood Is a Four-Letter Town*. Chicago: Henry Regnery Company, 1976.

Balshofer, Fred J., and Arthur C. Miller. *One Reel a Week*. Berkeley and Los Angeles: University of California Press, 1967.

Basinger, Jeanine. *Shirley Temple*. New York: Pyramid Publications, 1975.

Bogdanovich, Peter. *Alan Dwan: The Last Pioneer*. New York: Prager Publishers, Inc., 1971.

Bogdanovich, Peter. *John Ford*. Berkeley and Los Angeles: University of California Press, 1978.

Burdick, Loraine. *The Shirley Temple Scrapbook*. Middle Village, N.Y.: Jonathan David Publishers, 1975.

Cary, Diana Serra. *Hollywood's Children*. Boston: Houghton Mifflin Company, 1979.

Cooper, Jackie, with Dick Kleiner. *Please Don't Shoot My Dog: The Autobiography of Jackie Cooper*. New York: William Morrow & Company, 1981.

Day, Beth. *This Was Hollywood*. New York: Doubleday & Company, 1960.

Day, Donald. *Will Rogers.* New York: David McKay Company, Inc., 1962.

Eby, Lois. *Shirley Temple.* Derby: Monarch Books, Inc. 1962.

Gold, Victor. *I Don't Need You When I'm Right.* New York: William Morrow & Company, Inc., 1975.

Goodman, Ezra. *The Fifty-Year Decline and Fall of Hollywood.* New York: Simon and Schuster, 1961.

Goodman, Walter. *The Committee: The Extraordinary Career of the House Committee on Un-American Activities.* New York: Farrar, Straus and Giroux, 1968.

Gussow, Mel. *Don't Say Yes Until I Finish Talking: A Biography of Darryl Zanuck.* New York: Doubleday & Company, Inc., 1971.

Hays, Will H. *The Memoirs of Will H. Hays.* New York: Doubleday & Company, Inc., 1955.

Kanfer, Stefan. *A Journal of the Plague Years: A Devastating Chronicle of the Era of the Blacklist.* New York: Atheneum, 1973.

Ketchum, Richard M. *Will Rogers—His Life and Times.* New York: American Heritage Publishing Company, 1973.

Martin, Pete. *Hollywood Without Make-Up.* Philadelphia and New York: J. B. Lippincott Company, 1948.

Minott, Rodney G. *The Sinking of the Lollipop.* San Francisco: Diablo Press, 1968.

Reagan, Ronald, with Richard G. Hubler. *Where's the Rest of Me?* New York: Duell, Sloan and Pearce, 1965.

Selznick, David O. *Memo from David O. Selznick,* edited by Rudy Behlmer. New York: Viking Press, 1972.

Seldes, Gilbert. *The Movies Come from America.* New York: Charles Scribner's Sons, 1937.

Sinclair, Andrew. *John Ford.* New York: The Dial Press/James Wade, 1979.

Skolsky, Sidney. *Don't Get Me Wrong—I Love Hollywood.* New York: G. P. Putnam's Sons, 1975.

Smith, Patricia R. *Shirley Temple Dolls and Collectibles.* Paducah, Ky.: Collector Books, 1977.

Sobol, Louis. *The Longest Street.* New York: Crown Publishers, Inc., 1968.

Starr, Kevin. *Americans and the California Dream, 1850–1915.* New York: Oxford University Press, 1973.

Greene, Graham. *Graham Greene on Film: Collected Film Criticism, 1935–1939,* edited by John Russell Taylor. New York: Simon and Schuster, 1972.

Thomas, Bob. *Walt Disney: An American Original.* New York: Simon and Schuster, 1976.

Temple, Shirley. *My Young Life.* Garden City: Garden City Publishing Company, Inc., 1945.

Thomson, David. *A Biographical Dictionary of Film.* New York: William Morrow & Company, Inc., 1976.

Windeler, Robert. *The Films of Shirley Temple.* Secaucus, N.J.: Citadel Press, 1978.

Zierold, Norman J. *The Child Stars.* New York: Coward-McCann, 1965.

Index

NOTE: Film titles followed by dates
are those in which Shirley Temple appeared.

Index

221

Index